THE ELEMENTS OF
GARDEN DESIGN

THE ELEMENTS OF
joan clifton
GARDEN DESIGN

a source book of decorative ideas to transform the garden

photography by Jo Whitworth

aqua marine

Author's Acknowledgements

I would like to thank all the garden owners and designers who contributed to this book, for their generosity, hospitality, time and co-operation and for allowing their privacy to be invaded. Their energy and creativity sparkles throughout their accomplishments.

My admiration and thanks go to the project contributors who pulled out all the stops to devise and make original and stimulating features.

I owe immense gratitude to Jo Whitworth for her lovely photographs, painstaking attention to detail and fortitude during long, and occasionally uncomfortable, sorties into British weather.

I am indebted to Caroline Davison and give special thanks for her energy, enduring support, patience and unfailing ability to keep everything on track.

Thanks also to my family and friends for tolerating bouts of mental and physical absence, and especially to John Raffin for his infinite humour and support.

This edition is published by Aquamarine

Aquamarine is an imprint of Anness Publishing Ltd

Hermes House, 88–89 Blackfriars Road
London SE1 8HA
tel. 020 7401 2077; fax 020 7633 9499

www.aquamarinebooks.com; info@anness.com

© Anness Publishing Ltd 2000, 2005

UK agent: The Manning Partnership Ltd
6 The Old Dairy, Melcombe Road, Bath BA2 3LR
tel. 01225 478444; fax 01225 478440
sales@manning-partnership.co.uk

UK distributor: Grantham Book Services Ltd
Isaac Newton Way, Alma Park Industrial Estate
Grantham, Lincs NG31 9SD
tel. 01476 541080; fax 01476 541061
orders@gbs.tbs-ltd.co.uk

North American agent/distributor:
National Book Network, 4501 Forbes Boulevard
Suite 200, Lanham, MD 20706
tel. 301 459 3366; fax 301 429 5746
www.nbnbooks.com

Australian agent/distributor:
Pan Macmillan Australia, Level 18, St Martins Tower
31 Market St, Sydney, NSW 2000
tel. 1300 135 113; fax 1300 135 103
customer.service@macmillan.com.au

New Zealand agent/distributor: David Bateman Ltd
30 Tarndale Grove, Off Bush Road, Albany, Auckland
tel. (09) 415 7664; fax (09) 415 8892

Publisher Joanna Lorenz
Executive Editor Caroline Davison
Designer Larraine Shamwana
Production Controller Claire Rae
Editorial Reader Hayley Kerr
Stylist Gilly Love

Previously published as *Garden Elements*

10 9 8 7 6 5 4 3 2 1

Page One: A water barrel with playful sculpture.

Page Two: A metal figurative sculpture.

Page Three: A formal flight of steps (top left); a statue of a boy framed by pyracantha (top centre); formally clipped yew (top right); an informal pool edged with timber decking (bottom left); an Oriental-style bridge (bottom centre); abstract stone sculpture (bottom right).

Page Four: A weathered sundial.

Page Five: A decorative metal obelisk (top); a stone ball nestled in undergrowth (bottom)

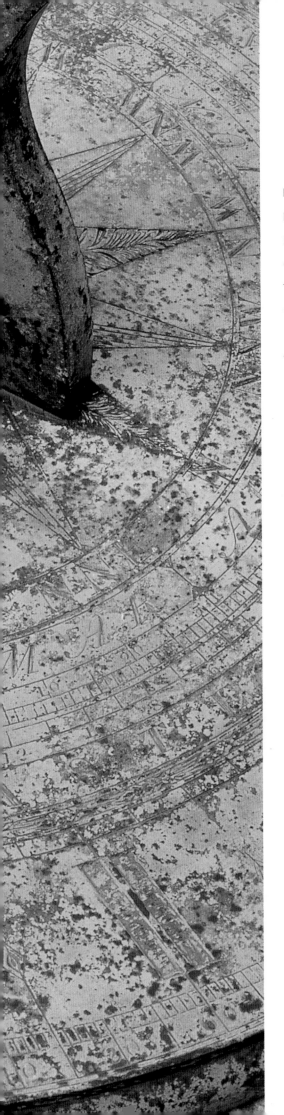

Contents

Introduction

Think of a garden as a very special kind of theatre. The trees and shrubs juxtaposed with walls, fences and paving make up the scenery, the plants are the actors, while the furniture and other features are the props.

A garden involves the interaction of plants with inanimate objects and forms. It can be purely a plant collection, an array of forms, textures and colours, all vying for attention. Plants change shape through the seasons; they increase in size; they produce flowers, fruits and seeds; finally their leaves change colour and fall. Perennials die down in winter, deciduous trees and shrubs sustain a framework throughout the year, while evergreens are constant features.

However, in order for gardens to be shown to their best advantage, plants need focus to emphasize their qualities. If you want a visually effective garden that will stimulate the intellect, permeate ambience and flair or even reveal a sense of humour, it is essential to consider the supporting elements. This type of garden has structure and form; it reflects the nature and architecture of its surroundings and includes features that give character and interest throughout the year.

This book examines the structural and decorative elements that provide a framework and focus in the garden. It takes you through the basics of form, shape and pattern, then explores the sensual qualities of colour, texture and sound, in the context of international styles, both contemporary and traditional. We visit grand, classical gardens with a view to learning new ways to adapt formal fashions from the past; we travel to the Mediterranean to find a relaxed style to reflect current informal tastes and the naturalist approach of the Japanese gardening tradition is opened up to reveal connections with organic and elemental philosophies for the 21st century. From rose-strewn cottage retreats to rugged Atlantic coasts, you will find a plethora of images to stimulate ideas for your own garden.

All the familiar elements or building blocks, suitable for the range of different gardening styles, are then explored. A wide variety of hard landscaping details, including paving, steps, bridges and tiling, are detailed in their various settings, and construction materials are described according to their suitability for each purpose. You will find lots of ways to bring water into the garden, with features

Above: **Terracotta floor tiles and steps provide a mellow background for this courtyard in which mature palms, olives and bananas are thriving.**

Below right: **Clipped balls of green santolina form an interesting geometric pattern which is reinforced at the rear by tall "lollipop" standard trees.**

Above left: **Sweeping beds of perennials and a stone cottage smothered with climbers epitomize the charms of a romantic garden. A vibrant colour scheme combines the red tones of** *Helenium* **'Moerheim Beauty' and** *Lilium bulbiferum.*

Opposite: **In hot sunny climates, pergolas can create welcome shade while giving support to a wide variety of fruiting and flowering climbers.**

varying from the formal to the bizarre. Different styles of furniture and planters are placed in context to help you create distinctive sitting spaces.

We aim to excite your interest in contemporary sculpture by revealing the work of talented artists, while an inspiring collection of projects, ranging from simple painting to more challenging joinery, will tempt you to have a go yourself.

Plants, hard landscaping and other decorative features all contribute an element of mass to a garden. The organization of these elements into a cohesive form will control the garden's balance and character.

form and shape

The form of objects is defined by lines and the brain is conditioned to perceive these lines in certain ways, depending upon their arrangement. Parallel lines, whether straight or curved, are orderly and therefore feel calming; cross them diagonally with another set of lines, and they become chaotic. Visual weight plays a part in this balancing act too. Placing a shape such as a square or circle at one end of the parallel lines focuses the eye on this point; duplicate the shape at the other end of the lines and the result is an equalization that creates a visual balance.

The shape of an object depends partly on its function and partly on the material from which it is made. Linear shapes, straight or curved, can be made from timber and steel or by cutting the material into sections, complex designs for furniture and trellis can be created. Clay can be moulded into bricks and tiles, or thrown on a wheel to make a flowerpot.

The circle, square and triangle are the primary shapes from which all other forms derive, and each has different characteristics. In plan view, a circle can create a central feature in a formal

Above left: **This stone ball is being drawn back into the earth by inquisitive ivy.**

Above centre: **A ball stands as a sentinel in the path, yet draws the eye to the stones on the left.**

Above right: **A steel spiral draws the eye upwards, giving an illusion of vertical movement.**

Opposite: **The strength of these evergreen shapes, emphasized by winter frost, provides year-round form and structure.**

9

layout, perhaps as a low wall or hedge to enclose a fountain, pool or statue. It can be set out as a linear detail in overlapping groups for an asymmetric paving design. Set on its side, the circle could form an opening for a vista through a wall or hedge. Pulled up, the circle becomes a cylinder, which might be seen as a structural column or as a planting container.

When the circle is massed up, it becomes a sphere; this can be set in concrete or woven in willow to make a sculptural feature. Spheres made from stone, timber or metal can be finials for gateposts or obelisks. Plants, such as box (*Buxus*) and lavender, can also be formed into spheres. The classic "lollipop" bay tree is a sphere on top of a tall stem.

The square, composed of straight parallel lines meeting at right angles, is the basis of formal design. It can contain a garden room with walls, or a parterre with hedges; it will enclose a central area to set off a feature or create a series of spaces.

The triangle's major role in the garden is in the vertical plane. Combined with a circle, it can be drawn up into a cone, which makes an excellent form on which to train climbers. It can be made from wirework or steel, which combine strength with visual lightness, or, for a more rustic effect, willow or timber. The cone is also a simple form for box or yew (*Taxus baccata*) topiary.

From the cone comes the spiral; this can be cut from solid plant material as topiary, or make up part of the construction of a climbing frame. Returned to the flat plane, a spiral can create a channel for a water feature, be formed in tiles for a mosaic or raked into pebbles for a Japanese theme.

Opposite (top): **The rectilinear form of this pool has been cleverly staggered both vertically and horizontally from the timber deck on which it is constructed. Energetic, blade-like planting creates a dramatic contrast to the smooth plane of water.**

Opposite (bottom): **The use of plants in an architectural capacity is shown clearly in this textural design. A narrow flight of stone steps is driven upwards by the trunks of tall palm trees, their dramatic fronds echoed by the spiky foliage of yuccas and cordylines.**

Top left: **The strongly directional form of this wrought-iron gate points the way to a group of soaring, columnar cypress trees in the distance. Tall bastions of closely clipped yew support the vertical theme, by lining the route towards them.**

Centre left (top): **Massed topiary with layers of clipped balls, wedges and pyramids shows the variety of forms that can be created from a single plant.**

Centre left (bottom): **The spiral represents an energetic life force, and this detail of a woven willow fence seems to spin like a newly lit firework.**

Bottom left: **Vertical blue spirals provide a dramatic contrast in form and colour to the low, tightly clipped santolina balls.**

Above right: **The vertical axis of the silver birch is crossed by the dark slate bench. The eye is drawn through by a succession of low green plant balls.**

Right: **An old yew tree has been tackled courageously to create a dramatic spiral.**

Patterns occur everywhere in nature, from the organization of leaves and petals to the striation of minerals in rock. They are the inspiration behind all our design theories.

pattern

Patterns comprise groups of marks arranged together in such a way that they create a picture. Variations in the shape and composition of the marks can result in endless permutations of pattern and design, whether they be geometric, abstract or figurative. These marks are usually defined as lines: wavy or straight, formed in circles or squares, arranged in groups of stripes, and set on the vertical, horizontal or diagonal.

Circles can be drawn out into a spiral – one of the fundamental life forces representing the energy of underground watercourses and the unfurling of fern fronds. The spiral formation of a snail shell has a mathematical formula that is repeated identically in all molluscs, and this shape occurs again and again throughout nature.

The complex patterns found on flower petals sometimes utilize dots and spots that serve to guide insects towards the pollen held on the stamens of flowers, rather like an airport runway. Used as part of a paving pattern, these patterns can perform a similar

Above left: **Round balls of bright green grasses contrast sharply with a glass "mulch".**

Above centre: **Patterns can occur naturally, as this *Melianthus major* leaf shows (top), or on manmade objects such as this piece of carved timber (bottom).**

Above right: **A pattern of stars within squares is emphasized by tall conical shapes.**

Opposite: **A parterre provides an opportunity to explore pattern.**

function by leading the eye towards a particular focal point or perhaps by emphasizing the way along a path.

Pattern in all its exciting variety may be used in hard landscaping in a number of different ways. Paving provides one of the most versatile opportunities. Suitable components are numerous, and the manner of laying further extends their potential impact. Bricks may be laid lengthways or on end, in straight lines, at right angles or in zigzag formation, each style resulting in a totally different visual effect. The incorporation of an additional element, such as slate, can form an edging border or serve to separate different pattern layouts.

Cobbles and pebbles are available in a wide range of sizes and shapes, including round, oval and square. Neutral colours from whites to blacks are cool and contemporary, and should be combined subtly to define the pattern. Cobbles and pebbles are also extremely useful where curved shapes are involved, and work effectively for centrepieces and pond surrounds. Pebbles used in a combination of colours also lend themselves to complex figurative designs where a distinctive focal point is required.

Exotic and complex patterns are often created with coloured glazed tiles, either cut into small pieces in order to make a mosaic, or left whole for larger-scale effects. Their fragility and poor wearing qualities make them most suitable for details on walls, risers of steps or tabletops and sculptural features. Our Mosaic Table project on page 108–111 may well stimulate you in this direction.

Top left: **An innovative archway made from a combination of willow and hazel creates a dramatic passageway to the woodland beyond.**

Below left: **Snaking spirals of small grey santolinas connect the domed mounds and lollipop standards of the topiary.**

Below: **This water feature was designed with great foresight in 1928. White railings, curved to enforce the visual gradient, frame successive flights of steps. The trunks of the silver birches reinforce the upward motion of the design and echo the rails, while the delicate foliage adds a sense of lightness.**

Bottom left: **Rectangular bands of violas contrast with narrow strips of green box hedging.**

Bottom centre: **The progression of a curved pathway between beds of thyme is indicated by a succession of Roman numerals which are set in circles amidst round stones.**

Bottom right: **Wrought-iron gates provide an excellent opportunity to contrast visual pattern with its adjacent planting. The spirals are a particularly popular choice among blacksmiths, and have an earthy resonance because their shape resembles that of unfurling plant tendrils.**

Colour is sensual; it evokes moods and creates atmosphere.
It can generate feelings of tranquillity and contemplation,
or it can produce drama and excitement.

colour

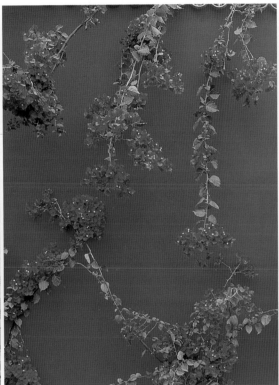

Colour can be used for instant makeover effects. Tired fences, decorative structures and furniture can be brought back to life with a coat of one of the new outdoor paints. Decorate dingy walls in shades of pale yellow to reflect light, or use ochre tints in a bright area to create a Mediterranean feeling. By choosing a shade like bright blue or deep purple for timber or metal furniture, you can create dramatic contrasts in a contemporary setting.

You can create an integrated colour scheme with toning shades to pull together disparate elements. Fences could be pale grey-green, with a pergola or arch in a deeper toning green. A shed could reflect the scheme by being painted in stripes of both colours or having window and door details picked out in one.

To unify a group of miscellaneous pots, paint them in a themed design like those in our project on page 116–117. Old watering cans and tin canisters can be given a new look, and old painted tools can be arranged together to make a colourful "found sculpture".

Above left: **The blue glaze of this stoneware pot contrasts with the red pelargonium.**

Above centre: **This Moroccan blue wall is criss-crossed with scrambling bougainvillaea.**

Above right: **The blue walls and pool edge create a rich foil for yellow pots and exotic plants.**

Opposite: **Rectangles of deep red plastic create a vibrantly hot theme, reinforced by brilliant orange flowers.**

Below: **The choice of pale blue paint gives this bench and planter a sophisticated air. It is complemented perfectly by the white standard rose and underplanting of petunias.**

Bottom: **The aged effect of peeling, pale blue paint combines beautifully with the pale terracotta of this Mediterranean urn.**

Instead of plain earthenware containers, plant bright pots for an exotic display on a terrace. Tiles and mosaics bring reflective glints as well as rich textures; use them on floors or on the surface of tables, to enliven old pots or as inlaid features in a wall.

Glass and acrylic plastic are exciting materials, having qualities of light transmission and colour absorption. They can be used to create water features or mobiles, or as translucent panels can be set into walls to give light without losing privacy.

Are you cool or are you hot? Make the effect you want to achieve by selecting the appropriate group of colours. Searing magenta and hot pinks, deep azures and glowing purples all suggest hot climates, cloudless skies and blazing sunshine. They are effective if you live in a sun-soaked southern environment, surrounded by elaborate tropical flowers with colourful birds and insects. These brilliant colours are wonderful if you want to be reminded of tropical holidays all year round.

On the other hand, bright colours can look uncomfortable in northern light under steel-grey skies. It is here that the pale shades come into their own; soft and elegant, they complement and support. Lovat greens and pewter greys give subtle contrast to foliage, while delicate lilacs and warm blues pick up the tones of flowers in the red/blue spectrum. They also work well in shady areas, glowing through and reflecting the available light.

The neutrals are cool and sophisticated. They are natural, with earth tones of clay and stone, pale creams through to soft browns. The deeper shades of grey and black, amber and terracotta strengthen the theme. Think of adobe houses in New Mexico, teak stilt houses in Thailand and stone houses in the Cotswolds. Each location is distinctive, but connecting them is the use of indigenous materials to create subtle and complementary buildings.

Above: **Pale blue furniture sits very comfortably among garden foliage. This subtly exotic scene is enhanced by the intelligent choice of lime-green fabrics for the cushions and parasol.**

Opposite (bottom right): **The soft mauve-blue of this fine wirework spiral makes a clever visual statement nestling among intense blue monkshoods and pale pink campanulas.**

The texture of an item suggests so much potential sensuality. From the smoothness of sea-washed pebbles to the coarseness of weathered stonework, texture brings a sensory dimension to the garden.

texture

Although touch is not absolutely essential to appreciate the qualities of texture, when your eye alights on an interesting surface, it is almost impossible to restrain yourself from reaching out to touch. How frustrating to find a notice beside a sculpture forbidding touch. It is like being denied the chance to experience the thoughts and the feelings of the artist.

Materials change entirely in texture and character, depending on the surface treatment that is applied. There is a world of difference between rough-sawn timber and carefully planed bespoke trelliswork. The smooth, sanded finish of an oak seat also reveals the high quality of the timber. When softwoods are painted, the natural grain is lost to view and the surface becomes smooth. If it is treated with a tinted stain, however, the grain and texture will still show through.

Granite, a massively hard and heavy rock, appears unyielding and aggressive when highly polished, but if the surface is given a lightly hammered treatment, it looks much softer.

Above: **A variety of different textures including rusting metal washers (top left); a spiral of crushed windscreen glass (top centre); a lichen-covered brick wall (top right); rough-sawn timber (bottom left); glass pebbles and deeply ridged mollusc shells (bottom centre); smooth pebbles (bottom right).**

Opposite: **An inventive mosaic of blue, glazed tile fragments highlights this maritime garden of smooth, sea-washed stones and spiky planting.**

Manufacturing processes can also change the texture and performance of the finished product. Stock building bricks are rough and absorbent, while engineering bricks feel hard, with a shiny resilience to water and frost. Similarly, hand-made terracotta pots feel pleasantly grainy, textured and mellow, while factory-moulded versions are shiny, with a rather dull appearance.

The same change can be seen and felt in metals. When iron is cast in a mould, the result is a heavy and lifeless article. Real wrought iron, a rare beast now, is pulled and hammered after heating and can be used to make decorative pieces of extreme delicacy.

Mild steel is also fashioned in this way, but does not possess the same flexible qualities or resistance to rust. However, a rusty surface has an attractively rustic texture which should be considered for an informal situation, looking very much at home among garden plants. Bright and reflective, stainless steel is smooth and hard. It has rust-resistant qualities and permits the clean, strong lines demanded by contemporary designers.

The malleable properties of soft lead sheet make it suitable for applied decoration and finishing, while cast lead is hard and less bendable. Zinc has similar qualities, although its appearance is initially bright. Steel may be dipped in liquid zinc for rust-proofing.

Clearly, the texture of materials chosen for the garden will determine its character and atmosphere. Shiny, hard surfaces are formal and metropolitan whereas rough finishes suggest a more casual feeling.

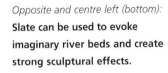

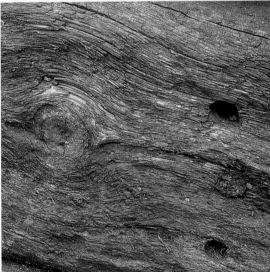

Opposite and centre left (bottom): **Slate can be used to evoke imaginary river beds and create strong sculptural effects.**

Top left: **Glass aggregate creates a reflective infill between beds.**

Above: **Shiny surfaces are smooth and bring reflective qualities to the garden.**

Top right: **Deeply veined hostas soften the edge of a rocky pool.**

Centre right: **Weathered wood has an interesting texture.**

Bottom right: **Grey and golden lichens adorn this stone finial.**

Below: **Tiny saxifrages contrast with the hard pebbles and the spiky pinks (*Dianthus*).**

Centre left (top): **A smooth ball contrasts with rough timber, fine gravel and glaucous foliage.**

Poplar leaves rattling in the wind, the sound of rustling bamboos, the splash of a fountain, the familiar chirp of singing birds – these are just some of the myriad sounds to discover and create in the garden.

sound

Because sound is invisible, it is usually overlooked as a dimension of garden design, but, used creatively, it can enhance and benefit your surroundings. A highly effective way of introducing sound is with water, which can be one of the most relaxing and satisfying sounds in the world. There is something very soothing about the gentle bubbling and flowing of moving water. It does need to be introduced thoughtfully, however: a vigorous splashing can be overwhelming, while at the other end of the scale tiny drips and trickles may become a trifle irritating. So remember to choose your water feature with care, especially if you have a small garden in which every splish and splash can be heard.

The presence of water will attract birds to the garden, so make sure that there are some shallow places for them to drink and bathe; these need to be safe from the attentions of local cats. The sound of birdsong gives us a real contact with the natural world and is a tremendous antidote to city stresses. To be woken in the morning by

Above left: **The sound of water splashing on to stones is both refreshing and enlivening.**

Above centre: **The "frothy" sound of this fountain suits the little floating figure.**

Above right: **Birds bring life and amusement to a garden; this frolicking tit is enjoying an exuberant toilette.**

Opposite: **Suspended slivers of carved Welsh slate combine sound with sculptural effect.**

the dawn chorus is something even town dwellers can enjoy, and it is comforting to hear the birds' evening song at dusk. If you want to attract birds all year round, remember to feed them regularly, especially in winter, when they are struggling against frozen ground and water, as well as the absence of insects and other natural foods.

Attention to the needs of wildlife in the garden can reap unexpected rewards for the ear. A snuffling and shuffling family of hedgehogs will be delighted by offerings of cat food. The buzzing of

bumble bees will accompany a mass of lavender and rosemary bushes. A squirrel, munching its way through a tree of green almonds, makes a spectacular noise, though not one that is always welcome!

Remember how much fun it was as a child to run and scuffle through a pile of fallen leaves in the woods? Leaves, tinder dry on the ground in the autumn, or fresh and shining on a branch in spring, offer a whole library of wonderful sounds. Even the slightest breeze will provoke evocative rustlings, while a good wind can produce howlings and rattlings worthy

of ghost stories. Plant trees with sound in mind. Eucalyptus, in particular, makes a spectacular noise, and if the main trunk is stopped a little above head level, it will develop a wonderful canopy of branches to suit even a small garden. Bamboos and tall grasses situated by a path also release lovely rustlings as you brush past.

Capitalize on the winds and breezes, and remember that a wind chime hung in a doorway or a mobile suspended from a tree branch can add another interesting sound dimension.

Opposite (top): **A lively fountain jet cascades over its bowl to trickle down to the pool below.**

Opposite (bottom): **A wonderfully textured Japanese feature has been created from an old cider press. The bamboo spout releases water, which trickles quietly on to the pebbles below.**

Left: **Wind chimes combine sweet sound with style.**

Below: **Still waters run deep, but not silent. Croaking frogs lurk around the pond edge and fish flap their tails on the surface.**

the styles

Style is a matter of personality, of understanding who you are. It is about character, not fashion; about creativity, not cost. The style of your garden is created by the way you see, feel and live. All your experiences affect your personality, and your garden will be a reflection of these influences.

In order to help you recognize and create a personal garden style, we have analysed the most significant aspects you need to consider. References are taken from history, showing how fashions over the centuries still influence ideas today.

Appropriate decorative items are suggested to complement the various looks, from rustic country garden to chic city terrace. From the guidelines offered, you will be able to piece together all the elements to realize your unique vision.

Plants, too, have their own individual, horticultural personalities, and we help you to understand the difference choosing the right plants will have on your garden. A thoughtful co-ordination of plants and the hard elements of landscaping will make your garden design a success.

Your geographical location will have a profound effect on your garden, from the point of view of both landscape and climate. We show you how to recognize the styles that will work best in your particular environment.

Cultural differences influence us when travelling, when watching films and when reading books. We look at important gardening styles from around the world, featuring gardens that are up to date with the increasingly popular minimalist style.

Opposite (top): **A low, pale-coloured wall surrounds a cool, Zen-inspired courtyard, paved with soft grey slate and creamy gravel. A simple planting of papyrus grasses and moss around the little pond is all that is needed to complete the sense of calm and tranquillity.**

Opposite (centre): **Vertical tree trunks and steel spirals emphasize the directional progression of the path in this formal town garden.**

Opposite (bottom): **Brilliant scarlet poppies pierce the early morning mist which so often envelops seaside gardens.**

Left: **A narrow channel of water bisects a path connecting two low fountains, creating a calming division between the mounds of exotic planting which surround it in this Mediterranean garden.**

formal

Garden design can be traced back to the Egyptians, but the landmark period of  the Italian Renaissance in the 15th century has influenced garden design until the present day. Classical form has been translated through the centuries, encompassing fashions right up to the contemporary designs emerging in the new millennium.

Below: **These symmetrical borders are emphasized by pairs of standard trees which are underplanted with clipped box. Elegant box pyramids punctuate the end of each narrow canal.**

The strictly rectilinear design is reinforced by the square-cut underplanting and horizontally banded background wall. The white wild boar acts as a focal point for the arrangement.

Centuries ago, powerful landowners commissioned the finest architects and landscapers to create their estates. Labour was plentiful and cheap, and technical skills in building were being developed, so it was possible to construct domains of staggering complexity and classical grandeur, which were imitated in successive centuries throughout Europe.

One only has to consider the vast scale of Versailles outside Paris, in France, with its huge earth-moving achievements, and the management and control of water in canals and fountains, to appreciate the skills and philosophies of its creator, Le Notre, which remain with us as inspiration today. The practice of clipping hundreds of topiaries and the transfer of dozens of palms and exotics in and out of the orangery at each turn of the seasons is still faithfully preserved.

The vastness of such estates demanded a supreme understanding of scale and proportion. Areas of land were divided by paths, avenues and canals; long flights of steps graced changes in level. These devices served to create the balance and form of the overall plan. The vistas

thus created formed long views through to statues and fountains, and provided elegant thoroughfares for promenading and games.

The smaller compartments formed between these paths were bordered by hedges of yew (*Taxus baccata*) and hornbeam (*Carpinus*) to emphasize their shape and containment. They are the forerunners to our current conception of the garden room. An exceptionally effective way to treat the traditional long, narrow plot is to divide it up into different areas, each one hidden from the next. In this way, the garden is revealed gradually as you pass through it, providing surprises and complete changes of look in a relatively small area. Even a tiny yard can be contained effectively in one single theme.

Formal gardens are perfectly suited to the metropolitan environment in which so many of us live. The constraints of small spaces set among densely packed houses and apartments can be exploited, because the presence of high walls and surrounding buildings gives privacy to your domain. The need for clarity among so many conflicting influences makes an ordered garden a calming solution.

Left: **Rhythmic pairs of trees create a rectilinear progression that crosses through horizontal canals. The clean trunks and square-cut box send a clear structural message in this contemporary garden.**

Above: **A handsome bench made from black slate rests on paving of black engineering bricks. The neatly clipped balls of box and helxine serve to offset the predominance of rectangular shapes.**

In town, shade is more likely, so white, scented tobacco plants (*Nicotiana*) or white busy Lizzies (*Impatiens*) would be perfect. Winter brings the possibility of cyclamen or heather to complete the planting cycle. This is an effective way to ring in the seasonal changes in a small garden, while maintaining the evergreen backbone and structure of the design. For a final

The parterre, a favourite planting device in the 17th century, is now finding horticultural favour again today. Within compartments enclosed by high screening, low hedges of box (*Buxus*) and aromatic herbs were laid out in curving or straight geometric patterns, known as knot gardens. If this seems daunting, make a simple arrangement of four compartments set in squares formed by low hedging. At the central point between them, set a focal point such as an urn, a sundial or a fountain.

In spring, bulbs provide an ideal infill within the squares. The combination of dark green box and white tulips is magical, while black tulips within silver-grey santolinas are sheer sophistication. In summer, in a sunny situation, you might choose feathery leaved cosmos, with huge white or carmine flowers.

Above left: **Low yew hedging and standard trees draw one inexorably towards a distant Gothic folly.**

Left: **Rectangular beds of grey santolinas, which have been clipped into tight balls,** **alternate with flat planes of lavender. The sophisticated and slightly surreal effect of the topiary in this parterre is further emphasized by the stocky little cones of box that sit at the corners of the low surrounding hedges.**

touch, the urn may be planted with a clipped evergreen, such as holly (*Ilex*), bay (*Laurus nobilis*) or box, or it may reflect the flower scheme of the parterre.

Topiary, or the art of training plants into shapes, has gone in and out of fashion since Roman times. It is currently seeing a fervent renaissance, and no self-respecting house in

London, for example, would be without at least a pair of lollipop bays set in Versailles planters at the entrance door. Architectural shapes like cones, balls and spirals always look smart and elegant, and will work well in both traditional and contemporary schemes.

Suitable plant subjects include the old favourites of box, yew (*Taxus baccata*) and bay, but many other shrubs and trees can also be used. Rosemary (*Rosmarinus*) and lavender (*Lavandula*) make good spheres; pyracanthas can be trained into shapes against walls; and even rustic hawthorn (*Crataegus*) can be given a sophisticated appearance by clipping.

Many familiar species take on a totally new character when pruned formally. Camellias and azaleas can be grown as hedges and trimmed closely with secateurs (hand pruners) in the

Above: **A circular parterre is divided into equal segments which are bordered by box hedging and focused at the centre by an elegant statue. This design formalizes the mixed groups of herbs making up the infill planting.**

Above right: **The segments of the parterre are focused at the centre by box cones. The mono species infill planting of lavender and sage has a calming effect.**

Right: **Yew obelisks lead to brick pillars and a summerhouse.**

Left: **Successive pairs of *Robinia pseudoacacia* create a rhythmic progression down this avenue.**

Below: **A graceful statue is framed by a tall beech hedge and a seasonal underplanting of brilliantly contrasting yellow wallflowers (*Erysimum*).**

Japanese manner, while box and pines (*Pinus*), Japanese holly (*Ilex crenata*) and common myrtle (*Myrtus communis*), spruce (*Picea*) and fir trees (*Abies*) can all be given the cloud topiary treatment revealed in our project on page 140–143.

Wirework frames are readily available to help you to shape and train your project. Wire is an exciting, flexible material that can be made into a host of other objects such as furniture, obelisks and trelliswork as well as

training frames for plants. The latter can be used to create instant topiary effects from climbing plants such as evergreen ivy (*Hedera*) in its numerous varieties or, in warm climates, the creeping fig, *Ficus pumila*.

Opposite (bottom right): **A classical terracotta urn makes a fitting statement before a rise of steps.**

Below: **A gambolling water lover makes an amusing feature.**

Bottom: **Formal containers make dramatic focal points.**

By training a flowering climber such as clematis or passionflower on to a shape such as a cone, it is possible to tame the unruliness of their natural habit while showing off the individual blooms to their full advantage. Combinations of clematis, such as pure white *Clematis* 'Marie Boisselot' with soft mauve *C.* x 'Lasurstern' are most effective, while the silvery seed heads of some of the species such as *C. tangutica* mean that they stay beautiful long after flowering has ceased.

Above: **Drama is created by a majestic pediment and a balustrade surmounting a steep progression of stone steps. The borders of box and bergenia that edge the flight of steps serve to emphasize the curving upward lines.**

romantic

Borders bursting with flowers of all sizes and colours, rambling roses spilling over a  wall, and chickens wandering in a potager filled with succulent vegetables: these are the images of country living. Whether in town or country, you can create a romantic idyll in which to lose yourself among the perfumes and flavours of the good life.

Romance suggests softness, abundance and fluidity. Rather than control the garden rigidly, create differently themed areas with informal links between them.

Of all the flowers, roses epitomize romance, and of all the roses, the old varieties, with their voluptuous, evocatively scented blooms, are the ultimate in sensual beauty. You can create a special rose garden to indulge yourself in all the gorgeous forms of flower. Groups that

In another area, make a garden focused on water. If there is a boundary wall, a simple spout through a lion's-head mask can trickle into a lead cistern below. In a more central position, create a round pool with a fountain spraying water droplets on to floating waterlilies (*Nymphaea*). For a stunning combination of deep blue and sulphur yellow, encircle it with a hedge of lavender surrounded by lady's mantle (*Alchemilla mollis*).

Hidden pathways suggest mysterious journeys. Create a tunnel of Japanese wisteria to allow the pendulous blooms to show to full advantage, or experiment with mixed honeysuckles (*Lonicera*) to create successive flowering and scent throughout the summer.

The romantic garden calls for a sensitive touch with furniture. It should be decorative as well as functional, making a creative contribution to the

include Bourbon and Gallica roses with names like 'Boule de Neige', 'Cardinal Richelieu' and 'Fantin Latour' are just so mouth-watering that they become irresistible. Colours from rich cream, through sugar-almond pink to the deepest purple, with perfumes to match, tempt you further into their trap. Give them lovely silver and blue companion planting to create seductive combinations that will extend the effect throughout the seasons.

Use pathways to invite discovery and allow them to meander between garden spaces. Soft bricks, old stones and cobbles all possess the required mellowness, blending sympathetically with flowers and foliage. In a wild area, where paving is inappropriate, mow a path through meadow grass. For spring, plant drifts of daffodils (*Narcissus*) and early bulbs, extending the colour from summer to autumn with successive sowings of wild flower seeds.

garden. Try to find interesting shapes that demonstrate delicacy or informality. The 18th and 19th centuries offer many romantic source references for furniture, with designs ranging from the classical to the fantastical. *Faux* rustic styles of furniture were popular at the turn of the last century, and can be suitable, made in either rough timber or hazelwood.

Fine wrought-iron and wirework chairs will combine sympathetically with soft planting schemes, and look fresh and original when painted in new colours; the colours used in our mosaic project on page 108–111 are soothing and subtle.

Painted softwood furniture comes into its own when the colour picks up on the flower theme; go for red-toned blues and grey-greens, which are good foils, or opt for the purity of white when total simplicity is required.

A seating arbour makes a lovely feature – the perfect spot for secret trysts.

It provides a wonderful excuse to grow perfumed climbers like roses, jasmine and honeysuckle, the theme of which can be continued along surrounding walls or trellis. It needs to be strong enough to carry the weight of the plants but still look delicate, so that it does not dominate the effect. The physical strength and visual lightness of wrought iron makes this a very suitable construction material; for an original look, paint it cream or blue-grey.

Opposite (left): **Folding canvas chairs are ideal for a hideaway.**

Opposite (centre): **A tiled-roof well echoes the house beyond. The profusion of purple clematis is another shared feature.**

Opposite (right): **Enjoy summer days on a rope-strung swing.**

Below: **Clematis-clad, bamboo trelliswork with symmetrical patterning creates a perfect backdrop to a border.**

The potager, with its mix of flowers, vegetables and herbs, is a romantic idyll to which many of us aspire. The taste of fresh produce that you have grown yourself and then picked will reward all your hard work and efforts at every delicious meal. There are so many unusual varieties now available that it is possible to bring new levels of style and flavour to your culinary endeavours in the kitchen garden. Ruby chard, purple curly kale and yellow tomatoes are just a few examples of the wide range of tantalizing colours and enticing textures now available to the vegetable designer.

When planning your space, experiment first on paper with different shapes and patterns. Straight lines make for efficient cultivation, but the plants do not need to be arranged in predictable rows. What works particularly well is a parterre arrangement, whereby you divide the area to be planted into four sections with a path running between them. Border each quarter with woody herbs clipped into little hedges; rosemary (*Rosmarinus*), thyme (*Thymus*) or sage (*Salvia*) would be suitable. Within them, arrange your planting design in radiating stripes or concentric circles, depending on the size and variety of subject.

If you have only a tiny space in which to develop a potager, it can be organized in a cartwheel form with triangles of herbs and salad leaves arranged between gravel spokes emanating from the central hub. Fill tall terracotta pots to overflowing with chives, marjoram and parsley, and group them in the corners. Utilize the vertical element with hazel tepees to support purple-podded peas, French beans (string beans) and decorative squashes, and form boundaries with trellises of runner beans (green beans) or blackberries.

Above: **A tepee of canes, densely clothed with climbing runner (green) beans, makes an attractive vertical statement among low-growing subjects.**

Left: **This potager at a French chateau is organized in an inventive parterre. It emanates sheer luxury and indulgence. The exaggerated use of mono species planting reveals the potential of form and texture in creating a design.**

Top right: **Vegetables that have strongly textured leaves, such as ruby chard and cardoon, are complemented well here by the red- and purple-leaved salad leaves. They are made even more effective by being planted in bold blocks.**

Right: **A simple ironwork walkway is transformed by a clothing of brilliantly coloured climbing nasturtiums and decorative gourds.**

Top: **Metalwork arches clothed with pink and purple roses define a pathway bordered by blue veronica and lady's mantle.**

Above: **Salvias, alliums and larkspur (*Consolida*) float in mauve drifts punctuated by** lime-green lady's mantle and red poppies. The result is a dreamily merging summer scene.

Top right: **A trellis arbour filters sunlight on to an inventive path made from sawn timbers infilled with pebbles.**

Top left: **Wirework chairs provide a vantage point from which to view these topiary peacocks.**

Main picture: **The unusual combination of flowering elder (*Sambucus*) with honeysuckle (*Lonicera*) acts as a frame for the farmland vista beyond.**

Top: **Swathes of *Geranium sylvaticum* barely leave enough space to walk through this romantic tunnel framed by an arch of trained apples.**

Above: **Pink climbing roses intertwine with fruiting vines over an old stone balustrade.**

mediterranean

 The pungent scent of herbs on a hillside overlooking the sea; bright, whitewashed, stone houses reflecting the heat of the sun; al fresco meals in shady courtyards: the images of the Mediterranean are heady and sensuous, wild and evocative. Friends sharing food and conversation around a table; gravel on the ground and terracotta pots filled with rosemary – it is a formula for easy living, relaxed but considered, comfortable but chic.

To achieve the shabby-chic effect, appropriate materials for paving would be rough stone slabs, hewn not sanded, or rustic terracotta tiles. Gravel suits casual areas or infill between beds, where there is not too much foot traffic; cobbles are effective for curved designs and path details. These all give the required appearance of rugged earthiness and will, in addition, absorb and radiate the heat needed by indigenous plants.

Old stone walls have the textural qualities to make an ideal backdrop, but they are only feasible in certain areas. A versatile alternative is to construct surrounding walls from basic building blocks, then coat the surface with a plaster render and finish it in masonry paint. Umber and sienna tones are warm and welcoming, while grey-greens lend a cooler, restrained quality. As long as initial preparation has been good, maintenance is not

A successful Mediterranean-style garden needs to combine a feeling of untamed nature with a sophisticated sense of colour and form. The effect is informal, but it results from the considered selection and positioning of the constituent elements.

In cooler climates, a sun-soaked area would be the wisest choice for location, making a sheltered courtyard to contain the design and enable tender plants to thrive. In hot and exposed situations, the inclusion of an arbour or pergola covered with vines will provide welcome shade and contribute creatively to the ambience.

In garden design, the groundwork and perimeters hold the various parts of the theme together and control the overall look.

a problem: crumbling paintwork is all part of the look. However, if you favour Greek-island white, be prepared to paint every year.

Mediterranean living is convivial and relaxed. To enjoy it with family and friends you need to sit and, most importantly, to eat. The table is the focal point around which these activities take place, so choose one large enough to spread with bowls of tomatoes and figs, plates of salami and baskets of bread.

The classic French-style garden table is made with wrought iron, with matching chairs softened with cushions. Alternatively, a more sturdy approach could feature a timber base supporting a stone tabletop or one covered in zinc, with generous cane-work bucket chairs for a really long lunch.

Top left: **Simple terracotta pots, bursting with pelargoniums, line a stone terrace framed with shade trees and tall cypress.**

Centre left: **Vertical stone pillars echo the tree trunks beyond and frame an ironwork pergola. The rectilinear form is reinforced by the stone paving and low perimeter walls.**

Bottom left: **Sienna-toned walls make a subtle backdrop to show off plaster reliefs, marble statuary and granite pillars. A gate in the background reflects the interesting ironwork chairs.**

Right: **The base of this octagonal marble pool is lined with pebbles to make a centrepiece for this thoughtfully planned, geometric courtyard design, composed of combinations of black, grey and white. Interesting use of colour and shape are used to indicate direction towards the gate.**

Below: **A lemon tree epitomizes the character of a formal Mediterranean courtyard.**

Below right: **Random stonework is organized into narrow squares in this shady courtyard.**

A little café table and a couple of wirework chairs would be perfect for an al fresco breakfast or an intimate chat over a bottle of wine. Junk shops (thrift stores) are a good source of old rusting pieces, often salvaged from parks and restaurants, and there are some exquisite new ones to be tracked down at design shops and flower shows.

Decorative colour features throughout the Mediterranean garden. Informal furniture, whether made from metal or wood, can be painted according to your mood or prevailing trends. Again, this is one of those areas where gently peeling layers of successive paint choices can add immeasurably to the charm.

The changes can be rung in quickly and inexpensively with different tablecloths and cushions. Provençal "Indienne" paisleys, for example, are stunning in combinations of blue, yellow and magenta; stripes are sophisticated in combinations of orange, green and taupe; and simple ginghams in pink or green are perennially fresh.

Terracotta pots must feature prominently in the Mediterranean, and the larger the better in order to cultivate the requisite clipped balls of box (*Buxus*) and bay (*Laurus nobilis*), or olives, lemons and figs if your climate permits. Containers tend to be most visually effective when used

Below: **This wooden furniture has a rustic charm that is well suited to the terrace. A canopy of dense climbers provides shade.**

Bottom: **Smoky pink walls and steps in this courtyard soften the effect of intense sunlight.**

Right: **A substantial timber pergola encloses a terrace with filtered shade and support for climbing plants. Wrought-iron furniture is fitted with soft blue cushions. Classic, circular, sprung metal chairs sit at the table.**

boldly and simply, in groups or rows of a single design, and the planting should ideally follow similar rules. Pots that are overflowing with a single colour pelargonium are classics for a balustrade or staircase, whereas on a terrace, a row of large pots might each support an orange tree or a huge ball of fragrant rosemary (*Rosmarinus*).

Depending on their source, clays can vary in shade from creamy white, common in France, to the deep reds of Tuscany. This will obviously make a considerable difference to the overall look, so it is very wise to consider your paving and walls before making a selection. Shapes include the straight, tapering camellia pots which are plain with a bold rim and the wide-rimmed lemon

Below: **The visual strength of this terrace lies in its utter simplicity. A row of matching terracotta pots, which are effectively planted with a single variety of pelargonium, lines one side. The furniture is unified by the choice of black wrought iron, while the pink granite tabletop reflects the soothing tone of the floor and columns.**

Bottom: **When the weather is warm and the sun is shining, it's impossible to stay indoors.**

pots, simple with two applied bands, or highly decorated with combinations of flower and fruit garlands, attended by cherubs and gods. Olive jars with narrow necks and bases make good architectural decoration or water features, but make planting difficult, as it becomes impossible to remove the rootball once the plant is established.

Glazed terracotta is a speciality of southern France, with mellow colours falling mainly into three groups: dark green, deep blue and mustard yellow. The tall Anduze vase, narrowing at the top to a low neck and at bottom to a plinth, is a classic. Try to find "antiqued" ones: the "aged" appearance adds to the effect. Other countries make glazed pots, but they tend to be of brighter colours.

Left: **Pale clay bricks set in a herringbone pattern pave a vaulted terrace. The stack of square terracotta "pots" makes an inventive rainwater spout to one side of the arch.**

Below: **The stone archway frames the view and provides a compelling invitation to pass through the wisteria-clad pergola beyond.**

Right: **Magnificently crumbling doors frame the entrance to the terrace beyond. These hand-made, Italian terracotta "lemon pots" are true Mediterranean classics. Although each contains a different species, the look is controlled by consistently using pots with the same shape throughout the courtyard.**

To complete the essence of fine Mediterranean living, why not also include a lemon tree to garnish thirst-quenching cocktails and an orange tree to embellish a healthy breakfast?

Flowering climbers adore hot, sun-kissed walls, and the choice of plants for these conditions is immense. However, it goes without saying that the iridescent bougainvillaeas are many people's first choice. Orange, bell-flowered campsis and the heavily perfumed white jasmines will also make an authentic contribution to a Mediterranean setting.

The character of plants in the Mediterranean garden is crucial to the authentic finish of the design. In their native environment they have to survive in poor soil, low rainfall and scorching sun, so their foliage and root systems adapt in order to cope. As a result, only a well-drained and sunny site will accommodate them. Textural grey and silver leaves are common, some furry and some spiky. Typical examples are *Santolina chamaecyparissus*, *Anaphalis triplinervis*, *Artemisia ludoviciana* and the prickly, thistle-like eryngiums. Immensely tall cardoons (*Cynara cardunculus*) produce huge, blue, thistle heads, which dry well for winter flower displays. Blue flowers look stunning among silver-leaved subjects, and none more so than the stately agapanthus.

Needle-like, water-retentive leaves, like those of the conifers, proliferate in the Mediterranean climate, and they also often give off pungent scents. Many herbs produce essential oils, resulting in foliage that is aromatic when crushed. Classic subjects include rosemary, sage, bay, marjoram and thyme. Fruiting figs (*Ficus*) and a grapevine (*Vitis*) to shade the timber pergola are real must-haves.

japanese

The setting is a hill-side covered in deep green moss, with paths winding past  contorted tree roots and rocks.

Clumps of tall bamboo rustle in the breeze; the delicate foliage of maples turns brilliant shades of vermilion in autumn, imitated by golden carp in gurgling streams. The feeling is of being at one with nature, a part of the living environment.

Japanese gardening is less about decorating the surface and more about what emerges from the earth. There is a sense of the energy of life forces, whereby rocks and tree roots are at least as important as leaves and flowers. The approach is a total reverence for the beauty and integrity of nature.

Although it is difficult to recreate this picture authentically outside Japan, it is possible to capture its essence. Simplicity, natural materials and integrity are the keys to success. Develop your own sense of organic form, using rocks, driftwood and planting. By all means, introduce a stone buddha or spirit house, but avoid the overuse of kitsch symbolism where possible.

Traditional Japanese temple gardens are situated in stunning, naturalistic settings of mossy hillsides covered in tall maples, their

Above: **This pine has been clipped in the traditional style of "cloud topiary" in which the growth resembles floating clouds. It is visually anchored by boulders and a box ball.**

Below: **This hut is just large enough for a diminutive gardener or a woodland god.**

sinuous roots clinging to giant rocks. Leaves turn every shade of gold and crimson in autumn, while lakes and streams are filled with exotic golden carp which flash in the sunlight. This method of garden design is known as "borrowed landscape".

Within the temple, garden areas tend to be focused to highlight particular styles or forms. These include bamboo plantations, background spaces devoted to maples, moss gardens, clipped topiary hedges and cloud pruning. The cascading blooms of trained wisteria are a special feature in spring, a time when overflowing cherry blossom creates an excuse for festivities in Japan. This season is so longingly awaited that weather forecasts include blossom reports all around the country.

Temples tend to be rectilinear, arranged with each room looking out across a

veranda to an individual style of courtyard. This "viewing platform" is used for meditation, often incorporated with the tea ceremony. The concept of composing a picture to view from the house translates effectively to the West, especially when gardening in a small space.

An unpromising courtyard, roof terrace or even a narrow balcony, can be transformed into a tranquil private space by incorporating some of the traditional elements. Enclose your area with combinations of dried bamboo screening and string-tied trellis to provide privacy and shelter. Plan carefully to make the best possible use of available space and concentrate on building up scenes of asymmetric balance using combinations of weight, height, form and texture, in both construction and planting.

Above: **A rocky outcrop is dramatized by this crashing cascade of water, descending to stillness in the pool below.**

Below: **A small, thatched retreat in a glade provides a contemplative veranda from which to enjoy the peace of this cool pool.**

Wood combines well with Japanese styling and is appropriate in the form of timber decking. An elevated seating area, leading from the house, can be designed with further changes of level to incorporate stepped planting and a small pool. Where space is available, an extended boardwalk could take a passage through the garden.

Plants with clean lines like bamboos introduce elegant form and delicate, rustling foliage; they exist in species of many differing heights and colours, including black stems and striped leaves. Blocks or borders of the black bamboo, *Phyllostachys nigra*, make a stylish living screen in milder areas. Ornamental grasses and sedges can also be incorporated, as can the prehistoric horsetail, *Equisetum trachyodon*. In shady, moist corners, simple moss and fern areas can be cultivated.

THE STYLES

Above right: **The tactile quality of these hand-sculpted boulders enhances their dramatic appearance. Here, they nestle among green sedges at the water's edge.**

Below right: **Rough timber planks form a sympathetic bridge across a shady pond; the clump of exotic plants and the bamboo water spout suggest a sort of watery oasis in the centre.**

Opposite (top left): **A sculpture of carefully balanced layers of flat stone subtly mimics the striated seedheads of quaking grass (*Briza*) that surround it.**

Opposite (top centre): **An impish Buddha sits smugly, wreathed in ferns.**

Opposite (centre left): **The spirit house is an important feature of Oriental garden design.**

Opposite (centre right): **The sight and sound of water surging through fern-covered rocks epitomizes the Japanese love of nature.**

Opposite (top right): **This handsomely carved spirit house makes a significant focal point between the garden and the woods.**

Opposite (bottom): **This brightly painted bridge makes a strong connecting statement between two parts of the garden. Specially designed gold finials emphasize the curve and movement.**

Evergreen, spring-flowering camellias and Japanese maple (*Acer palmatum*) for texture and stunning autumn colour can be sited individually or in groups. You can make your own specimen cloud topiary from box (*Buxus*) or conifers, inspired by the project on page 140–143. Stoneware is a traditional medium for containers, which can be sited in strategic spots. They are equally well suited to strongly textured palms and pines, or to clumps of ornamental grasses.

A sense of tranquillity and areas for contemplation are important elements in the Japanese garden. Water, the essence of all life, should always be present, and will help to create this ambience. In its simplest form, a stone bowl filled with water is calming, inviting birds to come and drink. In Japan, a spring would fill it via a bamboo pipe, and a bamboo ladle would be present to allow passers-by to take refreshment. This idea can be easily adapted into an attractive feature with the help of a small pump.

Moving water gives a sense of freshness and vitality. The effect of a stream washing over river pebbles would be a lovely idea, combining glinting reflections with the sound of bubbling water. A simple version would be fairly easy to construct using a shallow liner set beside a gravel path or decking. This could have water bubbling up through rocks that are piled up to just above water level at one end. The result is the soothing movement of water, without the need for a complex recirculating system.

In traditional Japanese gardens, paving is often made from combinations of pebbles and river stones arranged in geometric patterns, but, because of the natural irregularities of the material, the results have an informal quality. According to the source, colours vary from almost white, through pinks and greys, to almost black; the effect of rain extends these to deeper tones with a gleaming appearance.

The use of stones and pebbles is gaining interest in the West for both modern designs and less controlled rustic situations. Their rounded, irregular shape makes them ideal for circular designs and infill between planting areas. Although more expensive, whole pebbles are more pleasing in shape and texture than gravel; sizes range from 1–10cm (½–4in) in diameter, the smaller grades being most suitable for larger areas.

Rocks and stones have a special importance in Japan, with vast fortunes changing hands for prize specimens. The famous stone gardens, which some people consider to be cold and stark, are just one aspect of Zen Buddhist philosophy, but you can draw inspiration from them to create your own version. Choose some special stones of varying size, colour and character. Arrange them asymmetrically in one or two areas; uneven numbers of, say, three or five are best, and cover the rest of the chosen site with a layer of finer pebbles. These are then raked into variations of parallel lines and snaking spirals centralized on the main rocks. Clumps of green moss may be arranged around the specimens to provide a softening cushion, but to be completely authentic, no further planting should be included.

Opposite (top): **This Zen-inspired mask makes a striking statement surrounded by tall miscanthus.**

Left: **Adapted from a temple stone garden, this calm courtyard makes interesting use of sawn tree trunks to make paths through the gravel. Three handsome rocks stand sentinel over a tiny, bridged pool at one path's end, while the other leads to a sheltered viewing house.**

Below: **Bamboo wind chimes are attractive and create soothingly quiet sounds.**

seashore

Expanses of beach meeting crashing surf; sturdy little wooden huts painted ice-cream colours, all amid sand dunes and windswept grasses – this is untamed landscape, wild and free, beloved of artists and naturalists. If you have a yearning to break away, create the look in your garden and breathe in the fresh sea air.

Left: **Found objects can make excellent informal, and very often impromtu, sculptures. This still-life of rowing oars and a garland strung with pebbles sets an evocative scene against the timber-planked wall.**

Right: **Brilliantly coloured poppies make dancing shapes inside a circle of pebbles in this coastal garden.**

Below: **Pillars of stone-capped driftwood stand like maritime stalagmites among drifts of orange *Eschscholzia californica* and sea kale (*Crambe maritima*).**

The seashore recalls fun-filled outings and the exhilaration of bracing sea breezes, so why not make your garden a constant reminder of these sunny days by introducing elements of the seashore? When walking on the beach, especially in wild, exposed places, you can find exciting flotsam and jetsam washed ashore. Ropes, fishing nets, ships' timbers, redundant lobster pots and giant cable reels are all possibilities. These man-made objects can all be given a new lease of life, recycled in the seaside garden.

However, we must take account of our ecological climate when collecting objects from the seashore. Look, examine and take inspiration, but remember that shells, pebbles and rocks are part of a carefully balanced natural landscape, and we cannot just help ourselves. In fact, in many countries, collecting from the beach and the sea is illegal, even in tiny quantities, so please contact licensed suppliers, where you can source all the hard landscape materials you require.

Right: **Strongly textured agaves and eryngiums are softened by the delicate swathes of mauve-blue perovskias.**

Below: **This wide, flat beach-scape has been formalized by naturalistic parterres which are bordered with stones and flints. It is important to point out that cultivation in such a place is only possible with the incorporation of much organic matter. Sparkling, orange poppies provide just the right amount of colour to accent the pale, rounded hummocks of helichrysum and santolina and the yellow-painted window and door frames of the house.**

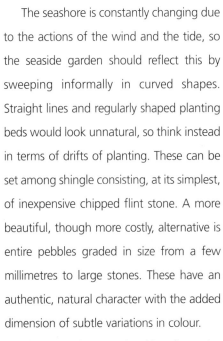

The seashore is constantly changing due to the actions of the wind and the tide, so the seaside garden should reflect this by sweeping informally in curved shapes. Straight lines and regularly shaped planting beds would look unnatural, so think instead in terms of drifts of planting. These can be set among shingle consisting, at its simplest, of inexpensive chipped flint stone. A more beautiful, though more costly, alternative is entire pebbles graded in size from a few millimetres to large stones. These have an authentic, natural character with the added dimension of subtle variations in colour.

Planting choices should reflect the windswept shore. There is a range of grasses to choose from, varying from short tufts to tall swathes. Graceful, narrow stems range from pale grey, through green to gold and white, with the added winter interest of seedheads that rattle in the breeze. This is an exciting group that will enable you to discover a new vocabulary of planting design with colour, texture, form and sound.

Safety and durability are important considerations when building out of doors. Decking must be constructed from durable hardwoods or specially treated softwoods. In moist climates, decks can become slippery and are prone to deterioration; boards with a ridged surface can help with grip, and so will regular brushing. Supporting structural timbers should be set in concrete, and no wooden part should be in direct contact with the earth.

To maintain the nautical theme, link the house to the garden with ships' decking made from timber boards. A raised terrace will make a wonderful sitting area from which to view the garden. You might also like to string out a canvas awning from the wall in order to shade the decking. This will make the whole experience of eating outdoors in summer much more pleasant. Changes of level and perspective can be achieved with timber walkways connected by steps.

Top left: **Natural associations work well in wild situations, as this seaweed fretwork shows.**

Left: **Beach huts could become sheds in a private garden.**

Above: **An elevated timber boardwalk makes a practical pathway across changing levels and boggy areas. It provides long vistas along the shore without disturbing vegetation.**

Maintain the timber regularly with a suitable preservative. Steps should be covered with wire mesh or incorporate a gritty, non-slip surface material. Ropes knotted through timber piers make effective balustrades and handrails; if there are small children be sure to add fixed, low-level, horizontal handrails.

The colours of this seashore style – faded blues like old denim and the greens of sea thrift (*Armeria maritima*) and seaweed – are

bleached by sun and wind. Textiles are canvas, duck and net, in plain colours or nautical stripes. Furniture is easy style: choose stripy deckchairs, swing a hammock between old ships' masts and make a feature seat from a rowing boat upturned on the shingle.

A garden shed can be transformed to look like a beach hut by painting it in vertical stripes of blue and white. If there is space, double it up as a studio with a veranda to make a private place to which you can escape and dream of the sea.

Top right: **Coastal buildings have to endure battering, salt-laden winds and strong sunlight. Preserved natural timber is relatively maintenance-free and unobtrusive in the seascape.**

Right: **This lovely chair is constructed from carefully chosen timbers which retain the shape of the original tree forks. It looks very much a part of the sea-washed landscape.**

contemporary

In our increasingly complex lives there is a growing need to simplify and edit.  The contemporary garden, pared down to pure form and texture, can create an environment that is both stimulating and calming, uncluttered by complex images. It is based on well-engineered materials, used concisely, and complemented by a focused palette of planting.

Left: **Changing levels have been utilized cleverly to provide a raised swimming pool and stepped planting beds, both formed from concrete. Steps tiled in terracotta are echoed in a perimeter shelf around the dining area.**

Below: **Bold steel tubes emerge from a pool, supported visually by the massive *Dracaena draco* and complemented by blue, concrete rectangles and square trellises beyond.**

Gardens are most successful when they reflect their surrounding architecture, so that house and garden complement each other. Contemporary gardens will therefore be most suited to buildings designed in the modernist period (1910–1940) or in the late 20th century. That said, any building of restrained formality might equally support such an approach.

The style is minimalist with an emphasis on simple forms, skilfully executed from quality materials. Advances in building technology have resulted in the emergence of many exciting new materials and special treatments to more familiar ones.

Steel, which can be polished and bright, stainless or rusted, may be used in sheet form, mesh and rod. It has a

multitude of structural and decorative functions, ranging from stairs and railings, arches and pergolas, to furniture and containers. Molten zinc is used to rust-proof steel, but in sheet form it can be made into containers or used to finish surfaces.

Concrete may be moulded into exciting shapes and finished with textured aggregates; it may be used for ground surfaces, walls and containers. Granite can be polished or hammered for use in walls and paving. Glass, mirror and acrylic plastic can all be used for screening or sculpture.

In today's gardens, much reference is made to the Japanese garden philosophy, so complementary natural elements such as stones and cobbles, timber and bamboo may be incorporated.

Left and above: **The versatility of modern materials makes possible the creation of complex designs. These nylon canopies, stretched between aluminium poles, are strong, practical and visually light.**

Right: **This highly charged water garden is constructed from insitu concrete with tiled borders. Gleaming, steel salmon leap and dance above the imaginary water.**

Top: **Simplicity of design, the effect of light and shadow and the versatility of concrete could not be better illustrated.**

Centre: **Steel wirework columns contrast with the yellow grid walkway above the pool.**

Bottom: **Horizontal limestone steps contrast with the strong vertical planting.**

Water is a crucial element in garden design, giving light, reflection, sound and movement. Combined with the imaginative use of construction materials in a contemporary design, water may be used to new and dramatic effect. Our contemporary water feature on page 152–153 demonstrates an innovative idea that you can easily recreate.

The balance of plants to hard landscaping means that their role is as much sculptural as horticultural. It is important to select plant material primarily with a view to its year-round architectural and aesthetic value, then be creative with form, making blocks and sweeps with single varieties. Select larger specimens, perhaps in pots, to make special features.

Plants with a strong vertical emphasis make good structural statements. There is a wide variety of bamboos available, ranging in height from 30cm–3m (1–10ft), with stems in colours from yellow and green to black, and with both variegated and plain leaves. Tall-growing varieties are excellent foils against high walls and make effective screening; shorter-growing species work well as an edging for paths. Tall grasses look terrific in large swathes, especially where there is some air movement to show off their sweeping habit. For infill areas, plant clumps of low-growing species with grey, hair-fine foliage. In winter, the grasses show off their shining, textural seedheads.

Opposite (right): **The terrace of a 19th-century building has been given a modern treatment.**

Below: **A cascade of water is disgorged from the massive, rust-painted screen dominating this small canal. The weight and form of the screen balances the presence of the nearby tree.**

Stately phormiums make tall clumps of narrow foliage in colours ranging from green to red-black, often with striped variegation; stunning, burnt-black seedheads stand on tall zigzag spikes in winter. Yuccas produce rosettes of narrow green leaves and a spike of huge cream flowers in late summer.

Succulent sempervivums have great sculptural value and are incredibly easy to maintain, needing virtually no soil and little water. They are best planted informally in gravel areas or in containers, where their low rosettes make an interesting contrast in scale.

The minimalist garden can be treated as a gallery space in which to display a piece of sculpture, or to experiment with exciting new designs of furniture and containers. The purist layout means that any object placed in it will be shown to full advantage, so take time to source pieces that are absolutely right.

It is refreshing to find designers who think especially of the garden when executing new ideas; specialist garden and decoration shows are a very good place to find them. It is now possible to commission a mirror-glass pyramid functioning as an accurately calculated sundial, around which you could base an entire courtyard design. Functional items are also taking on new forms: a steel and stone barbecue, so beautiful that it is almost a crime to cook on it, or a terrace heater shaped like a folding parasol.

Furniture made from aluminium and nylon, recliners formed from laminated steamed oak, and diminutive, acrylic plastic chairs all vie for attention. These are refreshing new concepts, often developed as lightweight, folding pieces suited to modern living and small spaces.

Opposite (bottom left): **A vertical, clear plastic tube allows an innovative view of bubbling water in this stylish feature.**

Centre: **A bold pink, concrete screen wall, through which a cascade of water descends, dominates this stylish pool. Horizontal elements of the house design are repeated through the doorway lintel, the water chute and the diving board.**

Below: **A courtyard is brought alive by a suggested water feature formed from transparent glass bricks and a "cascade" of mirror mosaic. Light is reflected into the area by the pale yellow walls and sand-coloured gravel. The foliage plants stand out strongly against the walls.**

Planted containers can be used as design features in their own right; you can reflect the pared-down look that is so popular among contemporary garden designers with tall and narrow shapes balanced with low, sculptural planting. Zinc, whether shining or patinated, and sheet-formed lead are the latest materials to find favour among garden designers. Made into simple rectangles, circles and tapering cones, they are both handsome and functional. Try making the container project on page 118–121; this enhances a simple timber planter by the application of a decorative lead grid. Concrete in innovative finishes and textures is also becoming increasingly sought after. Terracotta pots have always had a place in the garden; but it is best to choose oversized pots with any decoration limited to a simple rim.

the elements

Landscaping and garden design are exacting disciplines incorporating many layers of technical and artistic knowledge. These include horticulture, construction, history, ecology, fine art and spatial design. Creating the link and balance between these areas requires careful thought and judgement, and, as we have demonstrated, even the tiniest yard will benefit from special attention to detail.

Having seen a range of different garden styles, you may now feel that you have sufficient information to decide on your personal garden style; you may even have considered the planting and prepared a design plan. Once that is done, you can concentrate on all those detailed elements that, when brought together, complete the overall picture.

Researching suppliers, choosing objects and dreaming up special effects is a time-consuming business, and the information in this book should help you to short-cut some avenues by analysing the possibilities. A selection of suppliers and sources is included on pages 156–157. This is a creative area where you can have lots of fun, and we try to make it as interesting as possible for you.

Structural installations combine practical, architectural and decorative roles; by making the most appropriate decision about their design, your garden will have greater impact and become more enjoyable. The spatial contribution of steps, bridges and vertical structures are discussed and an examination of the

Left: **The use of architectural foliage gives immense presence to this Japanese-style courtyard, combining well with the substantial timber decking and the wooden pergola. The yellow parasol is echoed by the yellow flowering spikes of ligularias. This is an excellent example of how sophisticated attention to detailing can make all the difference to the look.**

Above: **A romantic wirework arbour makes an eye-catching centrepiece covered with** *Solanum jasminoides* **'Album'. The intricate design of the cast-iron bench completes the scene.**

Above right: **A flight of ancient steps is defined by the planting of pelargoniums. The alcoves of statuary provide visual relief and lead the eye to the terrace above.**

appropriate materials made. The contribution of pattern and texture when laying paving and tiling is covered. The designs and materials suitable for furniture and containers are assessed, to enable you to make fitting choices.

There is currently a fast-developing interest in the role of sculpture in the garden, with new galleries and parks opening all the time. This exciting and complex area is covered in some depth, with many photographs of exciting contemporary work that you can view and acquire. However, should you feel the creative urge to make your own piece, ways are suggested for you to reconstruct found or recycled objects. The horticultural artist is catered for as well, with ideas for plant training and still-life.

A broad range of exciting projects, from the very simple to some requiring a little more expertise, has been specially commissioned from a variety of talented artists, using a variety of different materials, from willow to wood, from metal to mosaic tiles. Full details of the materials and tools that are needed for these projects are set out with the method of construction. You will surely take a great deal of inspiration from these and endeavour to recreate some of them, or you may prefer to use them as a basis for your own individual interpretation.

Top right: **Alternate bands of sawn timber and pebbles are simple to lay and make a striking pathway through this timber pergola walk.**

Below right: **Black river pebbles laid on edge boldly centralize a mixed media design of pebbles, stone and brick, creating a change of texture within a foliage planting design.**

The function of paving in the garden is much more than simply providing a surface on which to walk. Paving can be likened to the floor and carpet of an interior room. Inside, flooring is chosen to complement wall coverings, curtains and furniture; outside, it must work with the architectural style of the house and its materials, the garden boundaries and planting. The feel of it under foot is important; is it smooth or lumpy, slippery or safe? Can furniture be placed on it without wobbling?

paving patterns

Below: **Concrete paviors meander across a sward, making a visual connection between the main house and the guest suite, without interrupting the natural flow of the garden.**

Bottom right: **A sensitive placing of brick paving enhances the softness and movement of this perennial border. Mortar between the bricks is omitted to allow self-seeding, which further naturalizes the effect.**

Throughout history, paving designs have been used as a decorative factor in outdoor spaces. The Romans created complex figurative and geometric floor pictures with marble mosaics. We will deal with the complexities of mosaics separately, and concentrate here on the principles of making floor patterns with elements of coloured and textured material. This is a diverse area that includes brick laying, cobbles, gravel, timber, pebbles, stone and slate.

The choice of construction material will determine the type of effect that can be achieved, together with its suitability for its purpose. It would be pointless to lay

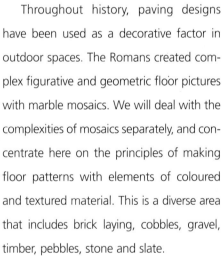

Its form is strategic to the overall plan and holds the complete picture together. An eclectic garden can be transformed by the unifying effect of a plain paving format, while a clipped topiary style would be enlivened by a clever pattern or texture.

Paths also have an important directional function, leading you through the various experiences of the garden. Terraces are gathering places to meet up with friends and family, places to sit or entertain.

expensive York stone in a wild garden, and in any case it would look totally out of place. In the same way, timber railway sleepers would look absurd with a period town house. Hard-wearing constituents like granite or cast concrete should be chosen where traffic is heavy, while gravels and cobbles are more suitable for areas where maintenance is not a major consideration.

The shape of the paving material controls the type of design that can be produced. One of the most versatile and

Left: **Positive channels of red brick cut through a riven stone path to emphasize the direction towards the steps in the garden beyond. An inspired border of eucomis boldly reinforces the statement and a red brick plinth for the distant urn completes the intended effect.**

Below left: **Timber decking is the natural accompaniment for this summerhouse in a seaside garden. Straight lengths of board laid widthways provide a sense of movement.**

High-fired engineering bricks are the most suitable for paving because they are very hard, strong and will not absorb moisture. Their slightly shiny, technical appearance normally lends itself to a formal situation, and the darkest purple-blacks can look elegant in a modern setting, perhaps combined with black slate. Softer, hand-made bricks are not usually recommended for paving, but their mellow qualities make them ideal for some traditional settings. As the bricks age, mosses tend to grow between them, lending a weathered air. Where possible, avoid cheap bricks, which are neither practical nor attractive.

easy to obtain is moulded clay brick, which can be sourced in a good range of colour tones, from reddish to grey-black. The rectangular shape lends itself to a multitude of combinations, and the colour tones can be introduced as part of the design. They can be laid in straight lines, at right angles and zigzags; laid lengthways or combined with insets of the short end face. A single line of a dark brick can form a decorative border to a path of another material such as stone.

Above: **Clay facing bricks are not really strong enough for use in paving, but they do lend a charmingly informal air to this cottage garden, complementing the materials as well as the age of the building.**

Left: **In large gardens, it is often inappropriate or too expensive to lay paving. Grass crisply defines and formalizes this island bed, while clear stretches of gravel provide the "white space".**

Above: **Changes of level are easily accommodated by the use of timber decking. Clean lines and restrained planting combine to create a tranquil pool area, linking a wooden terrace with the main garden.**

Below: **The herringbone arrangement of bricks makes a lively, yet informal, directional link through gravel in this romantic-style garden. The path leads enticingly to a well-tended lawn.**

Clay and terracotta tiles are the other popular pressed forms of paving material. Colours range from pale sand to bright red, depending on the source and firing method. In cold climates, ensure that they are fired at high temperatures to withstand frost and have them laid professionally to avoid cracking and breaking up.

York and other sandstones, limestone, granite and slate are gorgeous but costly. The beauty of natural materials is their variable colour, their patina and texture, which often shows mineral and fossil strata. They can be finished in different ways to change their appearance or performance and will mellow with age and use.

Sandstone and slate can be sawn into rectangular slabs, which gives them a very smooth surface while revealing the layers of colour tones within; in this form they suit fine architecture, both contemporary and classical. Alternatively, they can be split, leaving them with an irregular surface and edges resulting in paving with a less structured, somewhat ancient appearance.

Granite is one of the hardest-wearing minerals, and rectangular setts are one of the most popular ways of cutting forms for paving. These rectangular pieces are usually set end-on in concrete to reveal

a roughly surfaced square. Straight lines, diagonals or fans are the usual laying format, although their size and shape allow them to be arranged in circles. They also make good detailing features when combined with roundish materials like pebbles and cobbles.

Where budget is a consideration, it would be advisable to consider some of the better cast concrete replicas. Although some dreadful versions do exist, it is possible to source excellent versions of York paving, granite setts and terracotta tiles. You might be tempted by one of the aggregate mixes, which combine sophisticated textures and colours with excellent durability.

Concrete can be laid *in situ*, and if you have an artistic bent, you might like to experiment further with textures, patterns and eccentric aggregates. Concrete is supremely versatile and may be mixed with almost anything.

Informal and woodland situations provide an opportunity to experiment with timber. Horizontally sawn logs make great stepping stones through grass, and long sections of timber like railway sleepers (ties) can be butted up next to each other, perhaps with fine stones or chipped bark as infill between them.

Above: **The laminated texture of slate makes it suitable for using in wild, naturalistic designs. These borders are created from irregular pieces of slate, arranged vertically, whereas they are laid flat to form the surface of the path.**

Below: **Curves place special demands on the garden designer; the spaces around these square, brick shapes are filled in with an array of pebbles. The result is an interesting contrast of form and texture.**

bridges

Below right: **Rusticated stone slabs over a tiny brook blend sympathetically with the naturalistic planting.**

Centre (top): **Bridges serve an architectural role as well as a practical one. These spine-like timber balustrades move like an armadillo across a dried-up stream, accentuating the savage desert theme.**

Centre (bottom): **This bright lacquer-red bridge brings a touch of the Orient to a naturalistic landscape.**

Far right (top): **Fragile branches cut from adjacent woodland tentatively define the passage over a stream.**

Far right (bottom): **Timber is easily cut into sections to compose a variety of designs. The diagonal formation of this balustrade has enough understated sophistication to form a link between wild and formal spaces in this garden. The white paint effectively draws attention from the reinforced concrete bridge.**

When creating routes through a space, two different activities are taking place. One is directional, leading you towards an object or area; the other is spatial, separating one area from another. When these areas are separated by a change of level or by a barrier, such as water, a bridge can provide the route between them.

Visually dynamic, bridges can create a dramatic focal point. The famous wisteria-clad bridge over the waterlily lake at Monet's garden in Giverney is a classic example of a practical link made into a beautiful feature. The Victorians were enamoured with the Orient, and created a vogue for intricately designed Chinese-style bridges, painted brilliant lacquer-red. Such a flamboyant design looks dazzling, set against a naturalistic landscape.

As demonstrated in these examples, timber is a versatile construction medium. It is strong and can be cut into shapes to produce designs to suit a wide range of styles. It can be painted to complement or stand out from its surroundings, or it can be left natural, made in heavy sections of hardwood, and allowed to weather.

Alternative construction materials are iron and steel, which have great strength, enabling large spans to be created. This is often used to support timber in larger bridges. The versatility of metal makes it suitable for traditional and new designs. Sleek, contemporary forms capitalize on the qualities of steel and wire, which combine visual lightness and great strength.

Bridges across large expanses of water or big level changes call for specialist manufacture and installation. With water in the

garden becoming ever popular, there are a growing number of new consultants in this exciting field. In less demanding situations, it is possible to create a simple format yourself. To bridge a small stream or bog garden, bolt wide timber planks to cross struts fixed firmly into the ground on either side with posts. Safety is always important, so sling stout ropes between these to make handrails, and attach wire netting to the surface to reduce the risk of slipping. The level of sophistication can be adjusted by the quality and finish of the materials. At its most basic, rustic sawn timbers provide a woodland look, but more exotic hardwoods and careful detailing make this idea perfect for a Japanese-style situation.

The concept of straddling water can be brought down to even simpler formats, especially suited to small areas. For a contemporary look, concrete provides a versatile solution. The stepping stone concept can be brought up to date by casting concrete into blocks.

Where a small channel of water passes through an area of paving, straddle it with a reinforced slab. These are easy to make on site and you can use many tricks to lift the appearance. For a bright, clean look, replace Portland with white cement and sand. Aesthetic textured finishes can be achieved by applying aggregates such as gravel or grey-black river stones before the mix "goes off". These double as practical non-slip surfaces, but you can also scratch patterns on the surface once it has set.

steps

A sloping site can be a visual asset, but must be made manageable with terracing and changes of levels to enable circulation and easy cultivation. Conversely, a flat landscape can seem dull, and it may be desirable to excavate and landfill to create new shallows and mounds that will enliven the overall aesthetic. The practical way to move between these levels is by flights of steps. These should be thought of as not merely practical, but as making a sensory contribution to the design and or entrance. A grand flight of stone steps could descend from a classical balustraded terrace to a formal garden below; at the front of a town house, steps might guide the way to the entrance door, framed with clipped box trees in tubs. Natural stones such as granite or certain tough slates would be appropriate materials, and the surface should be textured to avoid slipping. Sandstones in their pale, mellow shades are always attractive, though less hard-wearing.

Above: **Informal landscapes demand subtly defined treatments. Mossy stone steps wind haphazardly up this wooded slope, taking care to integrate well with their surroundings.**

Above right: **Dark tree trunks, accentuated by the white gravel, form the risers of this slightly formalized woodland stairway. The carefully placed rocks fix the eye to a border of dramatic boulders on the right-hand side, asymmetrically balanced on the left by low evergreen shrubs.**

interest of the garden. Steps emphasize dimension and scale while incorporating texture and architectural effects.

Steps can add mystery because the ultimate destination may be out of sight. In a woodland situation, they might rise to reveal a clearing containing a sun-dappled pond with fish swimming lazily beneath the surface, or a sculpture positioned to surprise. In a topiary garden, they could lead down to a high-hedged parterre enclosing a secret seat or a fountain.

Steps can take a dynamic role in a garden, leading to an important focal point

Brick, which can be laid in a variety of patterns, also lends itself to formal designs, both traditional and contemporary. Durable engineering bricks that are hard enough to withstand wear and weathering should be selected. Available in burnished colours ranging from deep purple/red through to darkest grey/black, they make a handsome choice.

Practical and inexpensive, when concrete is laid *in situ* with care and attention to the finish, it is clean and functional and may be a good solution where lots of steps are needed on a limited budget.

In a small garden, it is likely that steps between levels will not have to travel very far, but every element has to work hard aesthetically. Turn a necessity into an interesting feature with three or four steps that are low, but wide and deep, to result in a gentle progression that has great presence.

Extended in scale, this style also works well over a long, shallow slope, with a series of shallow risers giving an elegant, gradual passage. The choice of material will

Left: **Architectural planting can transform the simplest stairway. This steep rise of grey stone steps is controlled by the bordering pyramids of blue-green conifer, and framed by an overflowing swathe of deep mauve *Ceanothus impressus*.**

Below left: **The imaginative use of materials enables the designer to create interesting effects. To create these rounded steps, the risers are formed from bricks set on end, with treads of tiles laid on edge.**

entirely control the finished look: cool and sophisticated when made from smooth, sawn sandstone, or rustic and informal with risers of timber railway sleepers (ties) retaining treads covered in gravel or chipped bark. This design can be further emphasized by placing identical planted pots at the same end of each step.

Small gardens depend on the vertical dimension to extend their space, so a run of wooden steps could lead to a raised terrace of timber decking. This could be sited with access from windows in the house, or to create a sitting space over storage sheds.

Above: **Sawn timber slats retain compacted earth steps covered with fine pea shingle. The bold borders of frothy lady's mantle (*Alchemilla mollis*) make an idea foil for this simple scheme.**

Left: **These red brick steps are defined by a row of matching terracotta pots beside a wall of Virginia creeper (*Parthenocissus quinquefolia*), contrasted with the lime-green variegated helichrysum.**

tiles and mosaics

A splash of colour can bring focus to a feature that might otherwise be mundane; when combined with a textural element, it gives the feature added life. Mosaics bring these two assets together, involving the creation of a tapestry from small pieces of coloured or textured material bedded into cement. The usual materials are tiles of glazed ceramic, glass, terracotta, mirror or marble, or broken pieces of any of these. The versatile nature of these materials makes them suitable for a variety of objects.

Taking inspiration from these ideas, it is easy to see how addictive this craft can be, though it is best used judiciously unless you live in a sunny climate that can carry brilliant colour. Our project on page 108–111 shows how mosaics can be used in a subtle way to bring a new dimension to a practical object. Makeovers like this can be made with many familiar items: old pots can be turned into new planters, while drinking glasses take on a new image as lanterns transmitting light through coloured glass tiles.

Above left and right: **The Romans were great protagonists of the use of mosaic in architectural design, providing inspiration for artists throughout the last millennium. This faithful reproduction depicts sea creatures using tiny pieces of marble and stone. Though they swim around a classical water feature, it is interesting to note how casually contemporary they look.**

The legendary Spanish architect Gaudi famously used mosaics to cover strangely amorphic shapes over buildings in Barcelona. Wildly curving balconies, chimney pots resembling warriors' helmets and curious mushrooms, all became his subjects. At his landscape development, Parc Guel, a courtyard meeting place is dominated by a long, snaking bench, aptly named the serpentine seat, which is covered over every surface with broken fragments of multi-coloured ceramics.

Try building a sculpture from chicken wire and cement. An exotic creature would be fun, perhaps a crocodile covered with multi-coloured scales. Three-dimensional objects may be quite demanding, but it is easy to create stylized pictures of birds or animals on a wall or to enliven a pool surround with tropical fish.

Mosaic can, of course, take on an ordered mantle more suited to quiet, formal situations. Examples can still be seen of Roman floor mosaics. There are countless

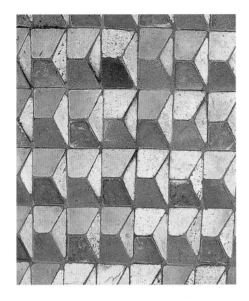

Top left and bottom left: **One of the most exciting aspects of formal geometric tile design is the huge variety of patterns that can be achieved. Although there are only two profiles of tile employed in this path, the arrangement of colours results in a dynamic three-dimensional effect.**

Left: **The balance of shape and colour controls mosaic design. Curious "push-me-pull-you" forms are framed by a background of cream shades.**

combinations of geometric forms, all based on the square, rectangle and triangle, which, according to their arrangement, result in linear, rectangular and circular patterns. By varying the medium, sophisticated results can encompass the understated pale tones of marble to black slate and burnt terracotta.

The influence of North Africa created Moorish Spain, with its palaces in Seville and Cordoba and the legendary Alhambra in Granada. Glazed tiles in geometric

patterns composed of a kaleidoscope of deep greens, blues, reds and yellows seem to cover every surface. In Portugal, tiles are used to cover the walls and floors of avenues, steps and even the lining of canals. In most gardens this would be overwhelming, so isolate small sections to reflect the image. A flight of concrete steps could be transformed by setting glazed tiles into the face of the risers; complete the Mediterranean effect with a succession of geranium-filled pots at each level.

Above centre: **The small size and random shape of mosaic pieces allow them to be used to cover odd shaped objects. This parasol stand has been transformed from the mundane to become an elegant part of the garden detailing.**

Above right: **There are many ways to use mosaics, as this rustic arbour shows. The panel depicting a flowering climber clearly demonstrates the subtle variations of colour possible when using glass as a medium.**

words and inscriptions

The carved inscription is understated and somewhat secret: it does not jump out but waits to be discovered. It can be provocative, propounding perhaps a philosophical idea or presenting a mathematical theory. It can be reassuring, extracting a meaningful line of poetry, or induce a smile with a frivolous remark. A memorial can mark an anniversary, evoking images of friends and family, or commemorate heroic deeds and landmark events.

Sculpture can take many forms, and the success of this subtle area is much dependent upon the quality of materials and the skill of the craftsman. Calligraphy is a most beautiful art which is fully developed when the choice of lettering style reflects the provenance of the inscription. The development of script has taken place over several centuries, each period and geographical location having an influence on the result. Whether whole poems or single thoughts are selected, a mathematical series or a simple house number, each gives an opportunity to test the understanding of the sculptor.

Minerals and stones from around the world have their own special qualities of colour, texture and density, and even individual pieces from the same source can show marked differences through the strata of which they are composed.

Above: **'Moonstone III' made from Penrhyn slate by Meical Watts.**

Left: **'Inceptis Gravibus' made from Welsh slate by Brenda Berman & Annet Stirling.**

Because the finished piece of work may be quite small, it presents an opportunity to select a really beautiful piece of stone with both visual and tactile qualities.

A piece of granite could take the form of a large beach pebble, pounded and smoothed to reveal its glistening mica; this might be picked up and stroked while its inscribed wisdom is pondered. A textured slate could be sliced to form a plaque for a wall, inscribed with a line of prose. A piece of limestone revealing tiny fossils, entrapped in a prehistoric age, might be articulated as a sundial, making an analogy with the passing of time.

Gardens are places to stimulate the senses and memories. How gratifying, then, to be reminded of a favourite poem while meandering through the garden. In the Scottish isles, Ian Hamilton-Finlay, a reclusive artist philosopher, has created a thought-provoking landscape, surprising visitors at watery vistas with architectural jetsam and rough-hewn stones. The siting and selection

Below left: **'Initial Posts' made from Welsh slate by Martin Jennings.**

Below right: **'Found Letters' made from Portland stone by Alex Peever.**

Bottom left: **'Hermetic Numerals' made from Welsh slate by John Das Gupta.**

Bottom right: **'WB Yeats Table' made from Welsh blue/black slate and Derbyshire limestone by James Salisbury.**

alone of these pieces is inspired, but when inscribed with thoughts and sayings, both disturbing and amusing, it becomes a holistic experience. So we see that inscribed pieces do not have to take a formal position. They can be settled in woodland or in a clump of bamboo, found nestling among grasses or placed beside a seat.

Stone is not a prerequisite, of course; when informality is more appropriate, concrete is ideal. Stepping stones cast at intervals through grass give an opportunity to tell a story; compose one and scratch it on the surface before the cement sets.

The vertical elements of the garden are an important aspect of its visual framework. They provide balance by making the link between the garden and surrounding buildings or large trees, or alternatively they give vertical scale in a level landscape. They may be a purely architectural statement or also provide an opportunity to grow climbing plants; in both cases they introduce further layers of colour and texture in combinations of materials and finish, foliage and flowers.

decorative structures

Top right: **A storage place for tools need not be purely functional; this pretty octagonal hut has been integrated with the rest of the garden by a pergola from which to suspend hanging baskets. The flame-red nasturtiums contrast well with the pretty shades of blue and mauve of the woodwork.**

moment to leave it natural and rusty. This is fine, as long as the metal is of sufficient weight: a flimsy construction will fall apart.

Any large structure made from timber should be made from adequately sized sections. Hardwoods need the least maintenance, and the natural grain looks best if it is treated from time to time with varnish or oil. Pressure-treated softwoods are a cheaper alternative, but if painted will need regular maintenance. Preservative stains, which colour the wood without obliterating the texture, are an alternative.

In its grandest embodiment, this feature would be a free-standing arbour, perhaps

The most appropriate materials for the construction of a framework would be metal and timber. The advantage of metal is its physical strength combined with a very light visual appearance. Although today wrought iron really means steel, it can be formed into very elegant shapes, and intricate designs can be made from wirework over a steel frame. To be fully weatherproofed, steel must be galvanized before it is painted, but it is quite fashionable at the

Above left: **A highly original lakeside pergola has been created on a concrete raft over the water. Constructed from wrought iron and glass, it encloses a metalwork throne.**

Left: **This romantic seating arbour is practically obscured by golden hop (*Humulus lupulus* 'Aureus') and a white rambling rose. Deep blue nepeta, which complements the mauve-stained woodwork, frames the picture with great style.**

making the focal point for a long vista. The romantically classical image is of twirling wrought iron or an intricate design in wood, painted in lilac blue or soft grey. However, it might also be formed in steel to make a contemporary temple, or in carved oak for a robust arts and crafts design.

A primarily architectural statement should be left unadorned, while a simpler framework would be ideal for climbers such as roses, clematis or passionflowers to complete the visual statement. If made

large enough to enclose a table and chairs, it can combine a practical function, making an elegant location for lunch or aperitifs.

At its simplest, a seating arbour enclosed by trellis at the back, top and sides can be easily placed, even in a courtyard garden. Used to support jasmine and honeysuckle, it makes a perfumed resting place. Lots of timber versions are available, but it is also possible to create more delicate looking designs from fine metalwork.

The arbour concept can be extended to that of a pergola, usually made from timber rafters supported on upright pillars. When attached to a house wall and erected over a terrace, a pergola clothed in climbers gives privacy and shade. Columns of steel or cast concrete make an elegant alternative support, where the architecture demands it. A less physically dominant effect can be achieved by stringing horizontal wires between walls; in this case, the plants have to do all the decorative work.

A free-standing pergola makes a gracious walkway to connect one area of the garden with another, or to frame a

Left: **An ebullient pair of silvery *Salix alba* var. *sericea*, trained into standards, is an inspired choice to frame this sentry-box-style arbour, just large enough to contain a chair. The frame, roof and trellis are made from timber that is painted a discreet blue-grey.**

Below left: **The birds have flown from this delicate Victorian wirework aviary, leaving it ready to be planted with a climber such as *Clematis orientalis* or *C. macropetala*.**

Above: **This enchantingly romantic arbour, set in a wild flower meadow, has been created from a combination of cast and wrought iron.**

Left: **Climbing supports make attractive architectural features to stand alone or bring contrast to a border. This wooden tripod shows off the clematis flowers in all their full glory.**

prominent feature. It is also a great way to grow a variety of climbers, alternating the species at each pillar so that each one has enough space and air. Both physical and visual strength are essential for this sort of feature: flimsy structures do not work. Thoughtful design, appropriate materials and competent installation are crucial to achieve the right scale and to avoid movement or deterioration.

The planted tunnel is gaining popularity again. Basically, this is a series of connected curved arches lining a path. This device is probably best suited to a large garden where it can be enjoyed only when looking at its best. When space does not permit such a grand statement, a single arch can be a useful framing device. By focusing the eye, it can direct movement towards a path or make an entrance feature in the opening of a low hedge or perimeter fence. The rose arch is the ultimate romantic image, but there are other flowering climbers to choose from that are equally beautiful and much longer lasting. For a permanent effect, ivy (*Hedera*) is the obvious evergreen, but in mild climates, a wider choice of species is available.

The garden gate is also an effective decorative structure in its own right. Reclamation yards are a good source of redundant objects that can be given a new lease of life, so why not find a wrought-iron gate and then create an opening especially for it? A tall hedge is a good subject for treatment; even if there is no access to the adjacent land, the openwork quality of a gate allows a view through to the scenery beyond. It also suggests spaciousness by hinting that there is a further garden to explore. You may have the opposite scenario, say an existing wall with an opening. Instead of choosing a ready-made gate from a catalogue, take the opportunity to commission one from the growing corps of artist blacksmiths who can create a design especially for your garden.

The obelisk is an essentially simple vertical structure, and by this virtue can be extremely versatile. It can be made in any height, be adorned with ornamental finials, and take on the related forms of the cone, pyramid or column. Obelisks and pyramids can be sited singly to give height in a border, in pairs to

frame a pathway, and in even numbers to enclose a formal parterre. The pure shape of cones allows them to be arranged in groups of three, or asymmetrically in varying heights, resulting in a dynamic sculptural statement. Columns may carry a pergola, frame a doorway or support an urn or sculpture.

If beautifully designed, obelisks can stand unadorned and alone. However, if they are destined to support permanent climbing shrubs, they should be strongly made from durable materials like metal and timber. Where informality is more appropriate, such as in the kitchen garden, hazel and willow tepees make understated but adequate supports for peas, beans and annual flowers.

It is advisable, especially in a small garden, to consider practicalities like the storage of tools and compost (soil mix). This could take the form of a long, low wooden box with a liftable lid, lined with resin or zinc for protection against damp. When a foam cushion is laid on top, it doubles up as a bench. Developing the idea, you can make it a structural feature built from bricks to retain a planting bed. By turning a second "box" at right angles, a seating unit is formed. The lid is made from timber, and the resulting corner space is perfect for a feature plant. A rectangular table completes a unit that is economical with space and cost.

A shed can be an interesting garden feature as well as a vital storage space. It need not be a major investment: the most basic design can be made to look smart when painted creatively. Try a *trompe l'oeil* of branches and birds or some fake windows with scenes of the potting shed inside. Even a tiny sentry-box style would look dashing painted in vertical stripes of colour.

Where space allows, a larger building is a luxury. If robustly constructed and insulated, it would double as a studio or children's den. A shingled timber roof would lift it from the commonplace, and with the addition of a shady veranda it would become a haven from which to admire the efforts of the day. The concept of a basic shed has thus been transformed into a garden room, expanding the scope of your garden both physically and visually.

Left: **A Victorian-style gazebo sits romantically at this lakeside, the scene framed by scented** *Philadelphus thalictrum.* **White-painted basketwork chairs complement the intricate design of the timber trelliswork.**

Above right: **This elegant gate provides an enticing glimpse of the garden beyond.**

Right: **These simple, timber obelisks give structure and height to an informal border.**

Willow obelisks can be used as architectural features in their own right or placed in pots so that climbers can be trained up them. Obelisks also act as focal points, adding height and structure to beds and borders. For an evening extravaganza, you might even like to adorn the obelisk with fairy lights to create a highly original decoration.

willow obelisk

Materials and Equipment

3 grades of willow:

4 corner poles, 2000mm (78in) long
and 18mm (¾in) in diameter

medium-grade willow for the sides,
13mm (½in) in diameter

thin pieces of willow for the twisted
base and ball (about the thickness
of a pencil)

willow clippings for the ball

pieces of wood for the support block

nails

hammer

drill

sharp knife

pair of secateurs (hand pruners)

chicken wire

pair of gloves

pair of pliers

linseed oil

white spirit (turpentine)

Preparation

Willow can be found in woods but it is advisable to check first if there are any restrictions on gathering material from local woods. A local wildlife trust or wood yard might also be able to supply you with material or at least advise you on where it can be obtained in your area. The willow comes in tied bundles which need to be soaked in the river so that they will be soft enough to work with. It should be soaked for one to two weeks, depending on the thickness of the wands and on the time of year, which will obviously affect the temperature of the water. If the bark falls off the willow when you work with it, then it has been soaked for too long. To test if the willow is pliable enough, twirl the tips around your finger several times. It should be soft enough to bend without cracking. If you do not have access to a stretch of water, you can also soak the willow in the bath tub. Drain the willow by standing the bundles up on one end.

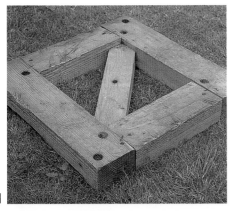

1 Constructing a simple wooden support block, like the one shown here, makes working on the obelisk easier as well as more stable than working directly in the ground. Use leftover pieces of wood where possible. The dimensions of the block are 350 x 350 x 90mm (14 x 14 x 3½in). Drill holes as shown so that you can create obelisks of two sizes.

2 Insert the four large corner poles into the wooden block. Sharpen the ends of each corner pole with a sharp knife, so that they can be pushed into the ground. Tie the poles together at the top. Twist the bands of thin willow about 230mm (9in) above the base of the obelisk.

3 Nail the twisted willow base firmly in place at each of the corners.

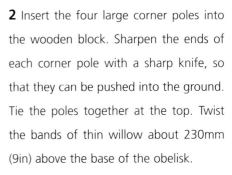

4 Using a pair of secateurs (hand pruners), cut points at the ends of the medium-grade wands of willow, so that they can be pushed easily into the twisted base at the corners.

5 Push the wands into the twisted base at the corners and weave two wands up each side to form a criss-cross pattern.

6 To create the ball on top, scrunch up some willow clippings and carefully wrap a piece of chicken wire around them. The wire can be cut with a pair of pliers. It is advisable to wear gloves to protect your hands from any sharp pieces of wire.

7 Gently squash the ball on top of the obelisk, pushing the tails of the medium-grade willow wands into the ball to secure it firmly on top.

8 Using the thin willow wands, start weaving through and around the ball in order to cover over the netting. The willow is fairly pliable, so this process should be quite easy.

6

5

7

9 Continue threading the willow wands through and over the ball until none of the wire netting is showing. The finished obelisk can be treated with a mixture of boiled linseed oil and white spirit (in a ratio of 50:50) in order to improve its resistance to poor weather.

8

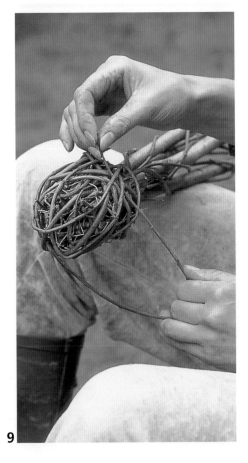

9

Right: The finished obelisk can be used as a decorative focal point just as it is or festooned with annual climbers, such as sweet peas (*Lathyrus odoratus*), during the summer.

garden furniture

Probably the first reason we place furniture in the garden is functional. A place to sit and a table to eat from are prerequisites. However, furniture plays a decorative role, too. A stylish bench, positioned at the end of a path, creates both an interesting picture and a reason to walk along to discover it; a tree seat further emphasizes the features of an important specimen.

Practicalities always have to be fully considered when working outdoors. If you plan to leave the furniture outside all year round, you must ensure that it is robust enough to withstand extremes of weather. The specification for the materials,

construction and finish needs to be very different from that of pieces for interior use.

The most obvious choice of material for outdoor furniture is wood. It feels and looks naturally sympathetic since it was once alive itself. Suitable durable timbers include slow-growing teak and oak, iroko and red cedar, the first two being by far the most beautiful and expensive. However, due to the enormous upsurge of demand for garden products, there is an increasing number of hitherto unknown

Top right: **French-style, ironwork café furniture is a perennial favourite. Its visual fragility and formal appearance make it ideal for courtyards and terraces.**

Above: **Obviously comfortable and robust, these teak chairs can be left out in summer to gain an attractive, weathered patina and then folded away again in winter. The table is sturdy enough to stay outdoors all year round.**

Above: **A stylish "Adirondack" lounger looks completely at ease on this wooden deck. The ridged surface of the handsome pot echoes the prominent veining of surrounding vegetation and the rhythm of the stripes in the timberwork.**

Left: **Cast aluminium is relatively light and rustproof. The verdigris finish camouflages this table and chairs beneath a weeping willow.**

tropical hardwoods on the market. Do support the cause of conservation by buying only those timbers that can be guaranteed to come from licensed plantation sources.

Softwoods grow quickly, so are easily sustainable and more ecologically sound. But they do not have the same qualities of durability or appearance. To help them last, they can be finished with preservative stains or painted. These finishes result in furniture that is more superficially decorative than those made from natural woods.

Left: **This imaginative swing seat has stood the test of time, hanging in an apple tree.**

Below left: **Oak is one of the most beautiful and enduring timbers, acquiring a silvery patina with exposure to the weather. This elegantly curved bench demonstrates how good contemporary design can also be classical.**

it has an incomparable feel of comfort and substance, the size can be a drawback for small gardens. In response to demands for choice, there is now a good selection of folding timber chairs and tables available. These have great flexibility of use because they can be put away during the winter or brought into the house to augment existing furniture when extra guests are expected. They also have a more contemporary appearance: chairs often incorporate elegant styling effects created by the interlocking of the parallel seat and back slats.

Timber can swell and crack when saturated with water, so the design of wooden surfaces should be slatted so that water runs away, instead of collecting in pools. Tables, benches and chairs formed out of solid sections are likely to have problems with their joints if no drainage feature is incorporated.

In order to sustain lasting durability, wooden exterior furniture has tended to be quite heavy and bulky. Although

Above: **In city courtyards, space is at a premium. Folding aluminium chairs are light and compact, and can be taken in and out in a trice. These two examples are smart enough to take to an open-air gala.**

Left: **The ubiquitous folding deckchair is practical and cheap. The addition of arms in this design makes sitting down and standing up much easier.**

If you are happy to have a table that is a permanent fixture, consider other natural materials. Slate and granite make magnificent tops that weather and age naturally; the surfaces can be either polished or hammered to a fine patina, revealing their subtle colour variations of greys, greens or reds. Although similar in appearance, marbles tend to break down too much and may also stain.

Stone tables are extremely heavy and impossible to move around, so if you are after something special, but a little more manageable, consider zinc. Just like for bar counters, it is used in sheet form and fixed smoothly over a wooden base. It is a very new look, smart, casual, and good for a contemporary terrace.

If these options are not to your taste, there are many other materials. For example, metal furniture has long been popular. It has a special kind of elegance, whether it be the fine, reeded, wrought ironwork of the Regency period or the cast-iron designs of Coalbrookdale, with foliage, fruit and flowers in sumptuous relief. Today, cast metal pieces are usually made of lighter aluminium.

Top left: **Intricate designs are a feature of cast iron. Fruiting vines decorate the arms and legs of this timber slatted bench, which is brought right up to date with a coat of soft grey-blue paint.**

Top right: **This curvaceous, wooden, arts-and-crafts furniture has taken on a lovely, silvery patina with age. It is subtly complemented by the antiqued wirework basket on the table.**

Above left: **A convenient pair of trees is not always available. This is a good example of an attractive, free-standing hammock. However, the cradle-like frame needs lots of space to work visually.**

Above: **In a tiny garden, every inch of space has to earn its keep. This brick and timber unit makes room for people as well as some fresh herbs.**

Opposite (top left): **A plank of timber supported on a couple of sawn trunks has just the right touch of rustication for a woodland rest-stop.**

Opposite (top right): **Enduring and weathered, this wooden bench doubles up as a workbench and display area.**

Opposite (bottom left): **A barbecue area beside a pool has been made from white insitu concrete.**

Opposite (bottom right): **Folding chairs are easy to move around.**

One of the most emulated metal chairs is the pretty French café design, utilizing curving lyre formations in the back with a woven slatted seat. It was developed from the bentwood furniture of the late 19th century. The other French classic from that period incorporates a circle of sprung metal segments in the seat and back, which incurve when sat upon; it is surprisingly comfortable.

Wirework furniture was also popular in Europe at that time and its popularity continued during the 20th century. Its beauty is its capacity to be curved and twisted into a multitude of shapes; it has a charming fragility, but is nevertheless strong. This versatile medium keeps enjoying revivals and examples can be found from traditional Gothic styles to 1950s funky.

However, it is in the realm of materials such as nylon and plastic that garden furniture can reveal its full potential. Often combined with aluminium frames, these materials are strong but light, making the furniture easy to move about. They can be translucent or opaque in a kaleidoscope of boiled-sweet acids to tropical hues.

When it comes to colour, we should not forget the humble deckchair: it is cheap, comfortable and bang up to date when covered with striped canvas. Directors' chairs can be found in smart canvas, ranging from grey and cream checks to navy and white stripes. If you have some tired old chainstore versions, freshen them up with a paint job and some wild fabric.

Garden seats for sitting are much more comfortable with cushions, which also gives an opportunity to update the look. Fabrics in plain colours, stripes and checks look the smartest; florals seem to be in competition with the plants, and not very successfully at that.

Hammocks are a fun form of casual seating. Made from canvas or crocheted string, they are just the thing for lazy weekends with a good book. They look best slung between two trees, where the occupier can benefit from the leafy shade. You can buy cradles to support them, but the effect of this contraption is rather contrived. Better to save up for a swing seat with an integral canopy; they even come in queen size, so there is no need to fight for possession.

tree seat

The beauty of this three-part tree seat, which is made from oak, lies in its simple design and the ease with which it can be fitted around a tree. The loose construction of the seat means that it can also be moved indoors during poor weather. For this reason, it can be built from seasoned or unseasoned timber. Oak can resist weathering without treatment for 50 years or more.

Materials and Equipment
for the 6 seat supports:

thickness: at least 80mm (3in)
height: to suit slope of ground, but a
minimum of 380mm (15in)
width: to match width of seat, but
tapered inwards at the top by about
25mm (1in) on each side

for the 3 seats:

thickness: at least 80mm (3in)
length: 1200mm (48in), 1500mm
(60in) and 1800mm (72in), depending
on size of tree and the available wood
width: 230–450mm (9–18in),
depending on the widths available
hardwood dowelling (sold in set
lengths), 12.5mm (½in) in diameter
mallet and gouge
metal ruler
handsaw
electric drill and 13mm (½in) drill bit
sharp knife (to whittle pegs)
waterproof wood glue
drum sander attachment
(coarse paper)

Preparation

Before starting work, check that the ground around the tree you have chosen is firm and well drained. If necessary, sink bricks or stones beneath the legs in order to provide additional support.

1 Using the mallet and gouge, chisel away the bark and sapwood from the wood around the edges of the legs.

2 Using the metal ruler and a pencil, mark the position of the legs on the underside of the seat. The first line should be about 90mm (4in) from the end. The distance between the two lines should match the width of the legs. Mark the edge of the wood to a depth of 25mm (1in).

3 Saw along the marked lines.

4 Create a 25mm (1in) deep slot at each end of the seat by chipping away the wood with the mallet and gouge.

5 Cut 12 pieces of dowelling to a length of just under 25mm (1in).

6 Drill two holes in the centre of the top of the legs, 150mm (6in) apart and 25mm (1in) deep, to hold the dowelling. Drill corresponding holes in the slots in the seat.

7 Glue the ends of the pieces of dowelling and tap in place in the holes on the underside of the seat.

8 Glue the other ends of the dowelling and slot the two legs in place. Hammer firmly into place, and wipe away any surplus glue. Level the seats into place.

9 Smooth the seat using the drum sander. Treat with wood preservative or linseed oil (optional).

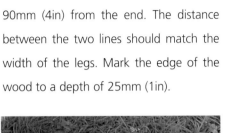

7

8

9

Obtaining Timber

Before deciding on the type of wood to use, it is advisable to visit a specialist timber supplier who can provide advice on a range of different woods as well as on their suitability for this project. Choosing the type of wood raises the issue of weather-resistance, durability and appearance. Preservatives can sustain the life of almost any timber, although hardwoods, such as the oak, do not need to be treated with a preservative.

The combination of colours and the simple design of this mosaic table makes for a striking piece of furniture. The table can be used outdoors in good weather, as it has some weather resistance, but you will need to bring it inside during very rainy periods and for the winter because it is not completely weather-proof.

mosaic table

Materials and Equipment

5 copies of the template on page 154

tracing paper and 2B pencil

drawing pin and string

masking tape

marine plywood or exterior grade plywood, 13mm (½in) thick

PVA (white) glue

paint brush

glass mosaic tiles in off-white, light verdigris, dark verdigris, moss, gold-veined verdigris, gold-veined green

tile nippers

goggles

flexible knife

cement-based, water-resistant tile adhesive

cement-based, water-resistant grout

small bucket

tiler's spreader

sponge and soft cloth

rubber gloves

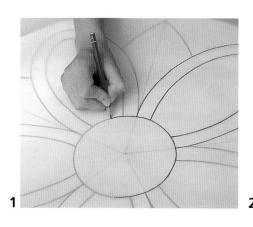

1

2

Preparation

Mark out the circumference of the table top, using a 600mm (24in) piece of string tied to a drawing pin at one end and a pencil at the other. Push the pin into the centre of the piece of plywood, then draw the circle, rather like a compass. Cut out using a jigsaw.

1 Enlarge the template, following the instructions on page 154. You will need five copies of this template. Cut out each template and stick together with masking tape to create the whole design. Using the pencil, trace the design on to the tracing paper. If the pencil markings are not strong enough, draw over them with a felt-tip pen.

2 Turn the tracing paper over so that the pencil lines are facing down. Place on top of the piece of plywood and rub over the lines of the design with the pencil.

3 Seal the board with diluted PVA (white) glue, making sure you seal the rim of the plywood as well.

4 Using the tile nippers, and wearing the goggles for safety reasons, cut the tiles into halves and thirds so that you have a variety of different widths. Make a small pile of each colour and save some whole tiles to nibble with the tile nippers into different shapes and sizes later.

5 Mix up the tile adhesive in a small bucket. Using a flexible knife, spread it over one area at a time, approximately 3mm (⅛in) deep. Select off-white, light verdigris, dark verdigris and moss-coloured mosaic pieces. Press them into the tile adhesive, leaving a tiny gap between each piece. Wipe away any adhesive spillages immediately.

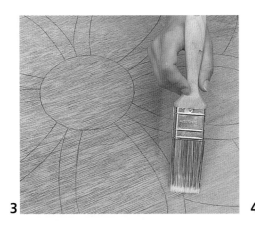

3

4

5

6

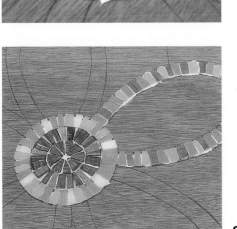

7

8

6 Fill in the area inside the ring with the gold-veined verdigris and gold-veined green mosaic pieces. In order to achieve a neat finish in the centre of the design, nibble the tiles into wedge shapes.

7 In the same way, stick down the outside rim of the rounded petal using the light verdigris, dark verdigris and gold-veined verdigris mosaic pieces.

8 Fill in the rounded petals with the light verdigris, dark verdigris, gold-veined verdigris and gold-veined green pieces. Nibble them with the tile nippers so that they fit neatly within the rim of the petals.

9 Fill in the pointed petals with the gold-veined verdigris, gold-veined green, light verdigris and dark verdigris pieces.

9

10

11

12

10 Fill in the area between the flower design and the edge of the plywood with the off-white, light verdigree and moss pieces. Leave to dry for a day.

11 Wearing rubber gloves, mix the grout in the bucket. Push the grout into all the cracks between the mosaic pieces, using the tiler's spreader. Wipe the tabletop and edge with a damp sponge. Polish with a soft, dry cloth.

12 When the tabletop is dry, turn it over and spread the base evenly with the tile adhesive in order to seal it.

Right and far right: **Pretty and light, this table is an ideal spot for relaxing in the summer.**

The container plays an important visual role in the garden, creating focal points among planting and emphasizing architectural features. It makes a statement of shape and form that is inseparable from the plants it supports. The container demands certain characteristics from the plant to complement it and the plant depends upon a certain style of container to set it off. The successful combination must then suit the garden setting. It is a balancing act of weight and volume with texture and style.

Above right: **A pedestal urn makes a good focal point for a parterre. Planting can be changed seasonally to alter the effect; this cascading froth of verbena and helichrysum makes an excellent horizontal balance to counteract the height of the display.**

containers

Right: **This refined and understated sheet lead planter makes a dignified showcase for white flowers such as this charming lily-of-the-valley (*Convallaria majalis*).**

Below left: **Lead can be cast in a mould to form a complex design. The octagonal shape is a good foil for the low-clipped laurel.**

Below right: **A bunch of iron-work rods has been fashioned into a stylish support for an unusual cone-shaped pot.**

material from which it can be made. Metals include lead, cast iron, wirework and zinc, and both hard and softwoods are suitable. Pure stone, moulded, reconstituted materials and concrete can all be used as well as the myriad fired clay and stoneware products.

The classic garden container we all recognize is the terracotta pot. These pots are made all over the world in shapes that include simple cylinders, Ali Baba urns and elaborate hand-made vases. The colour and texture differ, according to the source of the clay and the temperature at which it is fired: 1200°C (2200°F) is the

Containers look most effective when placed in an organized layout. They can be grouped together in a collection of varying heights and styles, lined out formally in a row of identical pots and plants, placed in pairs to frame an opening or positioned singly to balance another feature.

A "container" is any type of vessel that may be directly planted, or an outer jardinière to enclose one or more pots. There is barely a limit to the type of

minimum for any pot claiming to be frost-proof. If you live in an area that experiences freezing temperatures, do check that pots will withstand them. Colours range from pale creamy tones, through mellow umbers to rich brick reds.

The particularly special quality of terracotta, apart from a most sympathetic appearance, is its ability to breathe. Water and air can pass through the entire surface, so that soil dries evenly, not shrinking away from the sides. Terracotta also tends to

keep roots cool, and the overall result is that plants have a relatively stress-free existence, allowing them to grow better.

Impruneta in Tuscany is the source of what is widely considered to be the Rolls Royce of clays. The colour is normally deep umber to red, it has a very fine texture that minimizes water absorption (the main cause of frost damage), and it is exceedingly strong. These qualities, reinforced by superb traditional

craftsmanship and beautiful design, result in containers of classical beauty that will last a lifetime. They do, however, have a price tag to match, although many would consider them a justified investment.

The weight of these pots requires them to be hand moulded rather than thrown, and before being fired they may have a surface decoration applied. These range from a simple rim and border to elaborate designs including garlands of fruits, such as the famous "lemon pots", which can be large enough to contain a 3m (10ft) tree. In England, one pottery specializes in a similar manufacturing

Left: **The versatility of zinc is demonstrated in this coolly chic container. The tall, tapering form is contrasted by planting with a tightly clipped box ball.**

Below left: **This vase is a classic form suitable for placing on the ground or on a pedestal. Found in terracotta, carved stone and concrete, this vase is made from weathered, reconstructed stone.**

Above: **The combination of container and plant is a matter for great care. The spiky brown stems of this bamboo, together with a green glass mulch, perfectly match the patina and shape of the narrow stoneware pot.**

Left: **A carved terracotta urn displays lions supporting a pair of pensive cherubs.**

113

process, using a secret recipe for white Coadestone clay, an extremely precious commodity. This has many of the properties of Impruneta clay, but is even smoother, resulting in creamy coloured containers of incredible beauty.

At the other end of the scale can be found simple long toms, beloved of Victorian gardeners. This rimless, tall and narrow shape is finding much favour now for its simplicity and style. A kitchen garden would not be complete without some traditional pots, and rhubarb forcers make great decorations.

It should be noted that there is a world of difference between a hand-made and a machine-made pot. Hand moulding is described above, but the method of production with which we are more familiar is throwing by hand on a wheel. This method results in very lively pots that can be drawn up tall and narrow or squashed flat and wide. Although the exterior would be finished smooth, the inside shows the rings created as the pot evolves. If you look closely, you may also see the potter's finger marks. In contrast, machine-pressed pots tend to have a rather dead quality, shiny surface and uniform shape.

Terracotta, especially from the Mediterranean, is often glazed in deep green, amber or marine blue. These colours look especially beautiful in a sunny climate. Pots seen glazed in more brilliant shades are usually made from stoneware, which is a harder and denser material. Although lacking the natural porosity of terracotta, stoneware nevertheless possesses special qualities of its own, and large vessels made from it are highly prized in the Far East. It can carry complex glazes, pale green celadon being one of the most famous; the deeper greens and blues are beautiful too. In Japan, these pots are often fired in wood-fuelled kilns to create special effects in the glaze, particularly resulting in dramatic browns and blacks. In northern Europe, salt is often thrown into the kiln, producing a silvery brown effect on the surface of the pot.

These weighty stoneware containers lend an Asian influence to the garden and are easily able to carry expressive plants with architectural foliage. Bamboo, phormium, yucca, aralia and palms all make good subjects. Low bowls and curving jar shapes make stunning water features that reflect light in their glaze.

When an imposing kind of formality is required in the garden, the Versailles tub must come top of the list. Its cubic form and emphatic weight make it most appropriate for formal woody shrubs and small trees, which reflect its classical style and underline its mass. The sight of massed ranks of the original planters in the Orangery at Versailles is overwhelming; literally hundreds of pale grey-green boxes, in sizes from 50cm to 1.5m (20in to 5ft) tall, containing mature citrus, bay, dwarf pomegranates, conifers and palm trees, are taken in and out between summer and winter. These were designed with removable side panels to facilitate root pruning and soil conditioning, and it is occasionally possible to find new versions of these. Variations of this classic shape, more normally seen in sizes around 50–80cm (20–31in), are perfect for framing a formal entrance door; Paris and London abound with them, usually planted with bay trees or box balls. This is definitely not the container for frothy summer bedding.

Tall, narrow planters in round or square shapes are fast coming into vogue, their cool, understated lines being well suited to chic, contemporary living. Some very elegant examples are made from zinc, which reinforces their cool styling. For settings where this look would be too metropolitan, they can also be sourced in glazed stoneware, terracotta and wood.

To work well visually, tall planters must be planted sympathetically. Shrubs such as box (*Buxus*) in ball shapes, and rosette-forming architecturals like *Sempervivum*, give the impression of a low cushion, which artfully balances the tall form beneath. It is advisable to avoid oversized or flowing specimens that run the risk of being top-heavy. Note that these tall planters should be positioned out of the wind because their only drawback is their small base in relation to height.

Roof terraces present special problems for the container gardener, not least those of sun and drying winds, and the major consideration of weight. Containers fitted with automatic irrigation systems are crucial to avoid the necessity of watering continuously by hand, and wide-bodied shapes will help with stability from winds. In order to reduce unnecessary weight, planters made from plastics and glass fibre (reinforced plastic) are very useful options. Some excellent designs exist, although unfortunately they will never achieve the weathered patina of natural materials.

Left: **Roof terraces present special problems of weight and space. Zinc, a relatively light metal, has been fashioned into bold rectangles, large enough to support the production of vegetables.**

Top left: **The gently rusting patina of this cast-iron vase subtly reinforces the seeding grasses surrounding it.**

Top centre: **Rusty chain has been used very imaginatively here to create a textured beachside planter. The grass and pebbles perfect the design.**

Top right: **The beauty and endurance of high-quality terracotta is embodied in this old Italian urn.**

Elegant terracotta pots can be transformed with a selection of carefully chosen paint colours. Painting pots means you can introduce a splash of colour quite easily to any corner of the garden. An arrangement of three pots in different sizes is guaranteed to make a statement, particularly if they are all planted in the same way. The colours used to decorate these pots are cool and sophisticated.

painted pots

Materials and Equipment

3 clean, dry terracotta pots in decreasing sizes

paint tester pots in grey-green, sage green, pale lemon, orange and French blue

paint brushes in a variety of widths

exterior-grade varnish

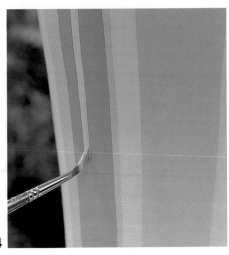

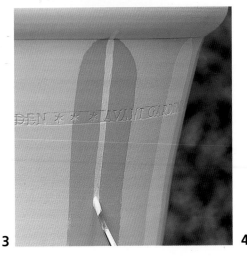

1 Paint the pot on both the inside and the outside with the base colour – in this case grey-green, but you can obviously design your own colour scheme. Apply a second coat as soon as the pot is dry.

2 Boldly paint stripes in sage green down the pot with a fairly wide brush, about 25mm (1in) wide. The effect will be more successful if you are as relaxed as possible.

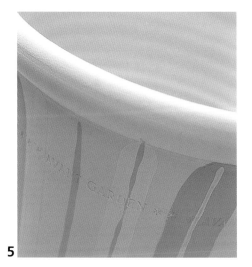

5

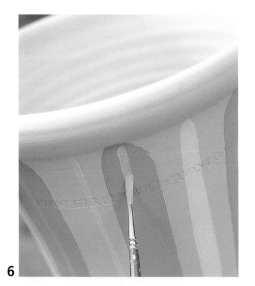

6

7

3 Paint pale lemon stripes using a variety of smaller brushes over the base colour and some of the sage green stripes.

4 Add the orange stripes.

5 Add the blue stripes.

6 Add stripes in the base colour on top of the remaining sage-green stripes. Repeat with the other pots. Keep standing back to check on the results of your labours.

7 Varnish the pots inside and out.

Above: **The pots look effective planted with the same plant, in this case a delicate bamboo with striped leaves. The layer of cobbles at the base of the pots adds a chic finishing touch.**

metal-trimmed planter

The lead strapwork of this timber-framed planter gives it a substantial, medieval look. The lead strips soon patinate to a lovely, whitish grey which gives the container an instant air of antiquity. The lead discolours with the effect of rain, but a white patina can be induced straightaway with the application of clear malt vinegar.

Materials and Equipment for a planter measuring 500 x 500 x 600mm (20 x 20 x 24in):

4 side posts, 50 x 50 x 600mm (2 x 2 x 24in)

8 side panels, 25 x 150 x 450mm (1 x 6 x 18in)

8 side panels, 25 x 150 x 500mm (1 x 6 x 20in)

4 base supports, 25 x 50 x 350mm (1 x 2 x 14in)

3 planks for base of planter, 25 x 150 x 445mm (1 x 6 x 17½in)

76 x 50mm (2in) screws

electric drill with a 5mm (¼in) drill bit

1 litre/1¾ pints/4 cups grey umber sadolin

lead strips (all 18mm/¾in thick):

4 side corner strips, 620 x 57mm (25 x 2¼in)

4 top edge strips, 510 x 65mm (20⅛ x 2½in)

12 horizontal side strips, 490 x 28mm (19¼ x 1⅛in)

8 vertical side strips, 610 x 28mm (24 x 1⅛in)

20 nails

80 galvanized metal pins

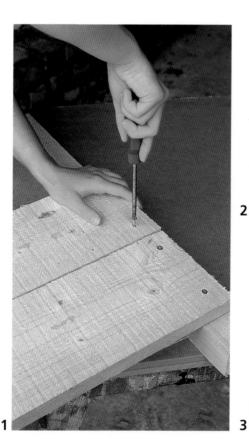

Preparation

If you are not confident of your wood-working skills, then simply purchase a wooden planter and apply the metal trimming, adjusting the measurements as appropriate.

1 Screw four of the side panels to two of the side posts, leaving 45mm (1¾in) at the bottom of the posts. Repeat for the opposite side of the planter, using the other two side posts and the remaining four 450mm (18in) side panels.

2 Turn over the panels and screw two of the base supports into position, using three screws for each support. The base supports should be flush with the bottom side panels.

3 Screw the four 500mm (20in) panels to each side.

4 Screw in the remaining base supports to the remaining sides, using three screws which are slightly staggered.

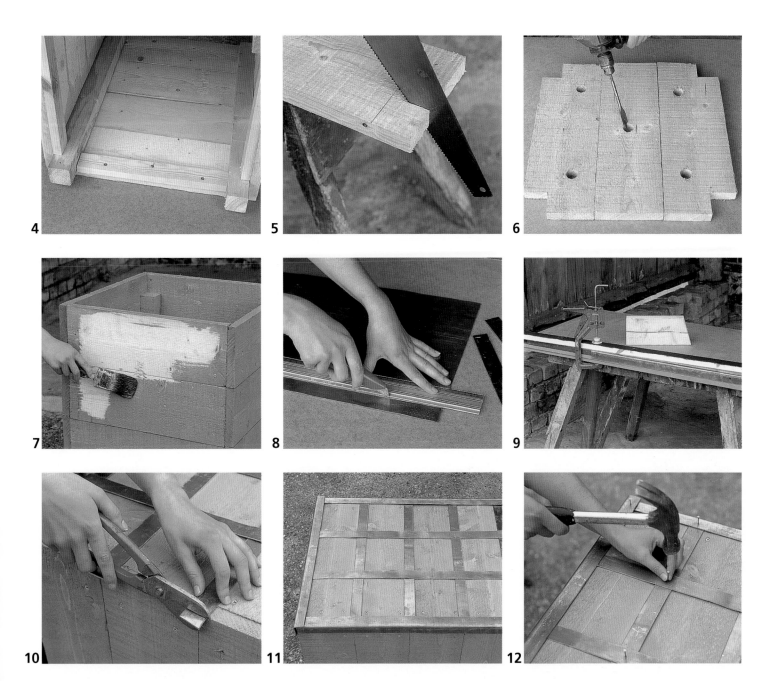

5 Using a saw, cut 50mm (2in) squares in the outer corners of two of the base planks. These will then slot over the corner posts and form the bottom of the planter.

6 Drill five evenly spaced drainage holes in the base planks, using the 5mm (¼in) drill bit, then slot the three base planks into position at the bottom of the planter.

7 Paint the planter, inside and out, with grey umber sadolin. Allow to dry. Apply another coat for a deeper stain.

8 Cut out all the lengths of lead strip, using a metal rule and a knife.

9 Place the 57mm (2¼in) wide lead strips into a vice as shown, and bend the strips down the centre so that they will fit round the four corners of the planter. In the same way, bend the top edge strips, but ensure that the split allows for 37mm (1⅜in) across the top and 28mm (1⅛in) down the side.

10 Lay out all the lead strips in position for one side. Position the horizontal strips first, laying them over the joins between the panels. Next, position the vertical strips, ensuring that they are evenly spaced – in this case, they are 125mm (4¾in) apart. Trim the strips down at this stage to ensure you achieve a neat finish.

11 Place the side corner strips and the top edge strips in position, starting with the corner strips.

12 Temporarily nail all the lead strips in place where they intersect, using a hammer and nails.

13

13 Replace each of the temporary nails with a galvanized metal pin.

14 Repeat the process of positioning and pinning the lead strips as well as adding the galvanized metal pins to the remaining three sides of the planter. Ensure that the vertical and horizontal strips are inserted under the corner and top edge strips.

15 Where the ends of the top edge strips overlap, cut into a 45-degree mitred corner as shown.

16 Using a wooden block, "dress" down or bend the edges of the top strips to form a neat edge at the top of the planter.

14

15

16

Right: **The finished planter contains a variegated holly that has been trained into a ball. The choice of plant perfectly complements the bold, rectangular shape of the planter.**

The garden offers a uniquely sensitive and sympathetic setting for sculpture. It can provide a naturalistic landscape from which a sculpture suddenly emerges, surprising the visitor with its unexpected appearance, or a more formal situation where the sculpture makes a statement that can be seen from a distance.

The word statue implies for most of us an imposing figure presiding over an important square or piazza. It is certainly figurative, usually representing human

statues

Top right: **Terracotta is a pleasingly soft medium for a woman poised romantically among an underplanting of white roses.**

Right: **A treasured statue should be displayed with pride, as is the case in this alcove.**

piece of sculpture is entirely subjective, and it cannot be overlooked that price must inevitably play a part in the decision. The degree of involvement by the maker and the cost of materials will have a huge influence on the cost of production; whatever budget you are working to, choose first for its craftsmanship, beauty and integrity. It may be far better to acquire a small bronze from an artist, to be set thoughtfully in a special position, than to give in to a large misrepresentation of Venus, cast in concrete, from the garden centre.

form and at least life-sized, such as Michelangelo's David in Florence. Classical gardens around the world have always placed statuary in key locations to emphasize the architectural plan of the landscape; they might be representations of soldiers and statesmen, mythological gods or characters from children's stories. They might stand alone or be part of a fountain.

On a domestic scale, a statue may have to be content with being somewhat less than life-sized. The selection of a

Left: **Quite small figures such as this patient angel take on a much more significant stature when placed on a plinth.**

Many makers of statuary advertize in the better gardening magazines; ask for brochures and visit them where possible to find the quality you want. Auction houses and specialist dealers are the best sources of antiques; with prices now reaching astronomical heights, it is essential to know the provenance and to be sure of the quality. Look out, too, for country-house sales and architectural reclamation centres where less prestigious items may be found among the serious treasures.

Left: **Dark green ivy provides a perfect backdrop for this refined carving of purest white marble.**

Below left: **A small stone figure set upon a tall column provides a sense of scale and emphasizes the change of level created by this flight of steps.**

weathering, it should look and feel as natural as possible when purchased, to guarantee enduring success in the outside.

Stone may be hand carved, although, because of quarrying and handling costs, this option is only really viable for smallish pieces. More likely, it will be cast in a combination of crushed stone and cement, or just concrete. This is the area in which most "off-the-shelf" work can be found; quality and style vary, but again, look for integrity of design and finish. Coloured tints and induced weathering are often incorporated to make pieces look aged.

Above: **A wall niche is an excellent feature of classical architecture in which to display a figure.**

Left: **A carved stone bust, elongated into a pillar, makes an excellent form to articulate the design of clipped topiary hedges.**

Basically, a statue may be made of metal or stone. The former will usually be cast in bronze, a beautiful but costly option, gradually acquiring a warmly weathered patina and improving in appearance over time. Lead is an alternative option with a cooler appearance; cast iron is also used, but less frequently. Cheaper representations can be found made from resin combined with mineral aggregates; quality varies, so consider the finish carefully. As there will be no further

animal sculpture

Above left: **Cats are always popular sculptures and this cast bronze beauty is no exception.**

Above centre: **These bronze storks look as though they have just landed in the shallow pond.**

Above right: **A pair of hares, cast in resin, gambol playfully in the undergrowth.**

Right: **A lifelike pair of swans prepares to take off from a waterlily-covered lake.**

Opposite (left): **The strange appearance of the guinea fowl is captured beautifully in this group of sculpted forms.**

Opposite (centre): **A wise, old owl, cast in resin, peers imperiously from his hideaway.**

Opposite (right): **Carved stonework is a good medium with which to represent classical creatures such as this lion and ram.**

Perhaps the most popular sculptures in the garden are animals. They are our friends and helpers, setting fine examples of courage and integrity. We may have a favourite domestic pet or be interested in a particular wild breed and wish to represent its quirky characteristics or fine breeding. Childhood memories are very important, too, and it is especially comforting to be able to commemorate an old pal who gave us so much loyal support in our early adventures.

For a city dweller, access to wildlife is very often limited, so it would be refreshing to introduce some. The sight of a gaggle of geese on the lawn would create a welcome illusion of space and freedom. Transported from the country-side, a lone sheep, grazing in the moonlight, might introduce an air of surrealism, while a flock of pecking hens brings the cosiness of the farmyard close to home.

There is plenty of opportunity with animal sculpture to be amusing and light-hearted without being over-cute:

the animals may be caught in silly poses or be constructed from informal materials. There is a current vogue for making shapes from coarse wire mesh, which is built up in layers to achieve the final form. The finished result, say a life-sized goose or a sheep, is

often dipped in zinc to galvanize it or even sprayed with red oxide. Wire is an extremely versatile medium, and most effective visually; it is practical, too, because it is heavy enough to be stable while still remaining relatively easy to handle.

Hollow wirework forms make ideal "living animals" when covered over in evergreen ivy (Hedera). These exist in a variety of shapes, including peacocks, swans and alligators; some hand-made pieces are even handsome enough to stand alone unplanted, as sculptures in their own right. It is even possible to acquire a life-sized, moss-filled deer, installed with an irrigation sprinkler ready to water the lawn.

Recycling comes into its own in all types of sculpture. An exciting collection of creatures ranging in scope from ostriches to tropical fish is being produced in Africa from that enduring standby, used oil drums. Exotic plumage stands out in dramatic steel shards while clawed feet dance and tail fins flash, all finished in burnished bronze hues.

Amphibians and fish are the perfect companions for a water installation. Choose from verdigris bronze frogs on lily pads, terracotta carp ejecting spouts of water or introduce a haze of metalwork mayflies darting from fine wires.

If you seek to deter predators from precious fish stocks, a tall crane cast in bronze might have the required effect, especially if you move it around from time to time to confuse the optimistic fishermen. Conversely, to attract migrating wildfowl, some decoy ducks floating on a large pond may encourage rare visitors from far distant places to drop in for a pondweed snack. If your pond is to their liking, they may decide to spend their vacation with you and even build a nest.

The transitory movements of wildlife are easily immortalized in sculptural form. A bowl where birds drink and bathe can provide a permanent rest-stop for a stone robin or sparrow; a row of starlings might take up residence on a wall, or doves spend their days among the roof tiles. Half hidden in a flowerbed, stone hedgehogs can lurk, waiting patiently for worms, and, by the lawn, an optimistic bronze blackbird might contemplate an oversized brass snail, in reality a cunningly disguised sprinkler.

Working with willow is a traditional craft and, although it can be difficult to master at first, making something from a natural material is really satisfying. This pig is made from a mixture of hazel and willow, both of which can be found in woodland. However, you may need to contact a wildlife trust to find the material you need.

willow and hazel pig

Materials and Equipment

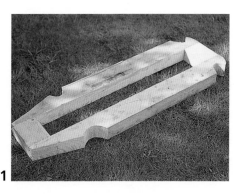

1

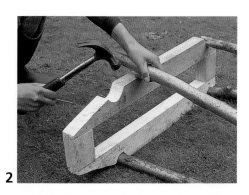

2

pieces of wood to make the pig frame, about 60mm (2½in) thick

1–2 bundles of willow, depending on how fat the pig is to be

4 hazel sticks, approximately 500mm (20in) in diameter

firm wire, 5mm (¼in) in diameter

8 nails, 80–90mm (3–3½in) long

claw hammer

electric jigsaw (optional)

saw

roll of chicken wire

pair of gloves

wire cutters or tin snips

pair of pliers

linseed oil (optional)

white spirit/turpentine (optional)

Preparation

Although the stripped willow, graded in different colours, that is used by basket makers is readily available, "rough" willow is used to make the pig. This means that the bark is left on the willow. A bundle or "bolt" of rough willow contains pieces of willow in different lengths and thicknesses. However, if you have to buy graded willow, then ensure that you ask for unstripped black maul which should be no thicker than a pencil and about 1500mm (60in) in length. You will need about two bundles of willow in order to make the pig. The pig's legs are made from hazel, and a bundle of hazel always contains 25 sticks.

1 Make the frame for the pig's body using the template provided on page 155.
2 Nail the four legs on to the frame as shown. You will have to get the leg slots cut out by a carpenter unless you can do it yourself with a jigsaw. Try to angle one of the legs to create a sense of movement and to make the final pig look as natural as possible. Saw off pieces of the leg if necessary to ensure that the pig will stand level.
3 Trim off a small amount from the bottom of each leg to make the trotters.

4 Cut out a rectangular piece from the chicken wire. It should be approximately 1200mm (48in) long, but the width will depend on how fat you would like the finished pig to be.

5 Turn the frame upside down and position it on top of the chicken wire so that the back of the pig is approximately 300mm (12in) from the bottom of the netting. You will need more netting above the top of the frame to form the pig's head. Cut small slits at the legs and bend the chicken wire around the legs.

3

4

5

6

7

6 Using a pair of pliers, cut and join the chicken wire down the stomach of the pig.

7 Shape the nose with your hands until you are happy with the effect. Leave a fairly large gap at the throat of the pig, so that you will be able to fill the head.

8 Stuff the nose first with willow wands and continue filling until you reach the pig's back. Continue to add layers of willow, weaving through the netting and building up the shape of the pig. Keep standing back and viewing from all sides to check that you are happy with the overall effect.

8

9

10

11

9 Bend and weave pieces of willow in circles around the legs and the muzzle.

10 Decide on the position of the ears. Push the firm wire into place and bend into loops to form the ears. Stand back to check the effect because unnatural ears create an unnatural-looking pig. Start weaving the willow around the wire to build up the ears.

11 Cut out a circular piece of chicken wire to form the rear of the pig. Attach the piece of chicken wire to the pig's rear, in the same way as you joined the stomach. Weave and thread more willow through and around the rear of the pig until no more netting can be seen. Attach the tail. This is the thin piece of willow that is usually used to tie the bundles.

12

12 Check all round the pig for bald spots and add more pieces of willow to fill in and create a neat top layer. The pig is not completely weather-resistant and will need to be sheltered in poor weather and during the winter. However, it can be treated with a mixture of boiled linseed oil and white spirit (turpentine) at a ratio of 50:50 to improve its durability. Before applying the mixture, ensure that the pig is thoroughly dry, otherwise the moisture will be sealed in, rather than kept out.

Above: **The pig makes an amusing ornament for the garden and one which both children and adults love.**

abstract wood and stone

All pictures: **Abstract forms look especially effective when set within a garden or woodland. Two of these pieces of sculpture have been hand carved by an artist, using stones or forest timbers, while the other two have been created from carefully chosen finds.**

Above right: **'Pictish Spiral Bench' in green oak by Nigel Ross.**

Right: **'Small Mound of Stones' by Ivan Hicks.**

The appreciation of art is a subjective matter, each of us having our own ideas of beauty and form. Like any form of visual art, sculpture need not be figurative and representational, but can be subtly suggestive or totally abstract. In fact, the natural surroundings of a garden make an exceptionally appropriate setting for such contemplative work.

In the 20th century, we came to understand a different kind of vision, where human and animal structure was pared down to reveal fundamental elements of form and emotion. In a world documented by photography and film, we no longer needed representational evidence of existence, but sought to expose inner feelings, idealism and spiritual beliefs. The work of Henry Moore and Barbara Hepworth forged an artistic revolution in sculptural expression. Moore's monumental carvings of stone and marble exhibit both power and sensitivity, while Hepworth's curving forms proved inspirational, suggesting a route that many artists have since followed.

It is interesting to reflect that, following this emotional subjectivity, a new form of "super-realism" is emerging, in which everyday objects are reassembled to challenge our casual acceptance of familiar surroundings and world events.

One of life's greatest privileges is to own a uniquely created work of art. A carefully chosen and positioned piece of sculpture can entirely refocus a garden

Left: **'Old Balustrades' by Ivan Hicks.**

Below left: **'Trunks' made from carved and scorched oak trunks by Giles Kent.**

design, giving a lifetime of pleasure. Knowledge of the artist and the inspiration behind the piece adds immensely to our appreciation, while understanding how it is made and the influence the choice of materials plays on the appearance and visual weight also add to the experience. Vastly differing styles of work can be viewed at a growing number of garden sculpture galleries and parks. You can learn about the artists and, if you wish, commission a work. International events such as the Chelsea Flower Show in London are also an excellent way to meet artists and view new work.

Stone and wood both possess attractive tactile qualities and each lends itself excellently to hand carving. Stone and marble are physically heavy, cool and hard to work. Their provenance and composition determine whether they take on a smooth, gleaming sheen or a rougher, granular texture when refined and polished. Though heavy, wood can suggest less visual weight and the appearance and feel are warm and yielding. Its character is revealed in the internal structure of graining and knots, and it is relatively easy to work.

The inspiration to create a piece of sculpture often comes directly from the shape and texture of the subject to be worked. Giuseppe Penone pares back vast building construction timbers to reveal the emerging branches and tree from which they were originally hewn. Ancient root burrs can be fashioned into huge, intriguingly "marbled" balls. An artist will visit the quarry to select a particular seam or colour, or selecting a specific piece of timber.

Even without any experience of carving, you can create your own sculpture with "found" materials. A strangely contorted piece of driftwood or an ancient vine might be an interesting object in its own right, or a collection of pieces can be assembled in any way you find pleasing. They can be sawn, drilled and nailed, burnt or even painted, if that will help to create your desired result. Experiment with different textures and combinations, perhaps incorporating other materials such as rope or stone.

Take inspiration from the Japanese Zen gardens with a collection of stones piled up in the form of a tall cairn. Flattish pebbles of varying colour and size make an interesting "totem pole" when balanced on top of each other. Larger pieces of rock might be arranged into a druid offering that emulates Stonehenge. The only limit to the effects you can create is your imagination.

abstract metal

Until the late 19th century, the concept of using metal to form sculpture was confined to the casting of precious materials such as bronze or lead into representational statuary. Today, the immense and powerful works in welded steel by Naum Gabo and Richard Serra have made truly revolutionary inroads into our perception of contemporary sculpture.

Gabo was an early 20th century Russian pioneer of "Constructivism", which involved building up sculptures

compose curving, narrowly parallel walls, reminiscent of a medieval souk, and seductively snaking circular enclosures of eerie and overpowering presence.

The use of steel for art makes sense when we consider the huge influence that this material has had on the construction of 20th-century buildings and transportation. There are many finishes and weights available for creative use. In a contemporary garden, polished stainless steel can be shown alone, in all

All pictures: **Metals take on a different character depending on the way in which they are made. Cast pieces have a high degree of density, while a lighter effect can be achieved by hand-working the metal into fluid shapes, such as leaves, or through the creation of airy assemblages of fine wirework.**

from simplified elemental parts. It was highly exciting for him to use the newly developed engineering techniques of riveting and welding to fix the weighty steel sheets together; famous work includes the huge but hauntingly beautiful "Constructed Head" series. Serra's recent work in the United States involves slabs of corten steel, 60cm (2ft) thick, 4m (13ft) high and up to 10m (30ft) in length. These are assembled to

its light-reflecting glory, or combined with water moving over its surface. Corten steel is intended to go rusty, but without staining or deterioration, making it a perfect material for combining with stone or concrete.

As we have seen, the word sculpture does not imply only an original work produced by a known artist. Sculpture need not be serious, and gardens can certainly benefit from a sense of mystery and fun. Scrap yards contain a stunning array of pieces of rusting metal and mechanical parts, just waiting to be recreated into forms from your imagination. It is tremendously gratifying to recycle a piece of cast-off junk into a personal creation. Pieces can be incorporated into water features, hung from tree branches or intertwined with plants. They may stand alone as a massive statement or materialize from a border to create a clever surprise.

The visual quality of rusted steel is a bonus, looking completely at home among vegetation. Stainless steel can be polished to a high shine, or textured to various matt finishes; it does not rust so will always remain gleaming. Galvanized steel wire is flexible and can be fashioned into a multitude of forms or simply used to hold other components together.

Other metals have interesting qualities too. Copper, available in sheet or wire form, oxidizes to a green verdigris patina.

Opposite (left): **'Butterfly Gate' made from galvanized steel by Victoria Rance.**

Opposite (centre): **'Organic Form' in copper by Peter Clarke.**

Opposite (right): **'King and Queen' in bronze by Helen Sinclair.**

There are no rules to follow when creating and devising your own piece of sculpture: anything that excites you can be employed in your work of art. Reinforcing rods, balustrades, gears and washers, engine parts or fuel cans, service pipes and air-conditioning ducts are all potential components; there is no end to the possibilities when you think laterally. Ducting and large cans can also be utilized to make eccentric planters.

Non-rusting, shiny aluminium sheet is flexible and can be cut with snippers. Zinc and lead sheet can be folded and pinned over a wood base. Titanium is gently reflective, taking on hues that mirror the mood of the sky and light.

This is a dangerous field in which to operate, so prepare equipment and protective clothing in advance. If welding facilities are not available, drill, wire and bolt lighter-weight pieces together.

Above left: **Detail of 'Cosmic Tree' in copper by Peter Clarke.**

Above centre and above right: **'Euridice' in bronze by Helen Sinclair.**

Not all garden ornaments need be on a large scale or last for a long time. This metal mobile, which is made from discarded aluminium cans, is a case in point and could be used to adorn a tree or decorate a seating area. Being made of metal, it will inevitably rust, but it makes an enchanting ephemeral ornament for the summer.

metal mobile

Materials and Equipment

2 x 440ml (15½fl oz) or 500ml (17½fl oz) drink cans (both must be the same size)

medium-grade sandpaper

sharp nail

hammer

pair of gloves

sharp knife

pair of scissors or tin snips

screwdriver or pencil

16–18 clear glass stones or nuggets

masking tape

adhesive (suitable for metal and glass)

680mm (27in) thin wire

key ring or curtain ring

1

1 Using the sandpaper, gently rub the cans to remove the printed finish and reveal the bare aluminium. Take care not to crush the cans while doing this. You might like to leave the cans unopened at this stage in order to provide a firm surface on which to press.

2 With a sharp nail and hammer, punch two holes in one of the cans at the 12, 4 and 8 o'clock positions. Remove ring pull.

3 Pierce the side of the same can with a sharp knife and, using the tin snips or the pair of scissors, cut away the bottom of the can. Trim any jagged edges. Repeat for the top of the other can.

4 Starting at the open ends of the cans, cut 13–18mm (½–¾in) wide strips to the bottom. You should have 16–18 strips.

5 Roll each strip around a screwdriver or pencil to create the decorative scrolls.

6 Roll some of the strips up and some of them under.

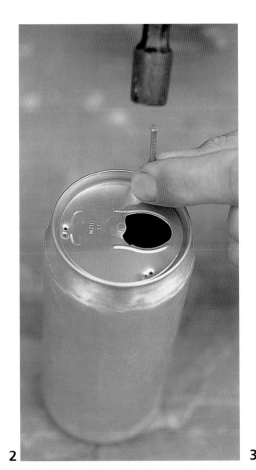

2

3

4

5

6

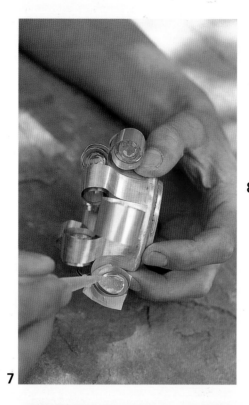

8

7 Fix one of the glass stones to a strip of masking tape, then gently unroll a scroll until it will fit around the stone. Using the tape to hold the stone in place, place a few drops of adhesive around the edge of the stone. Remove the tape as soon as the stone has set (after 30 seconds or so).

7

9

10

8 Continue to glue the glass stones in every other scroll.

9 Thread three pieces of wire, about 150mm (6in) long, through each pair of holes. Secure by twisting the ends.

10 Glue the two cans together, end to end. Once they are fixed, arrange the scrolls by gently bending the strips. Join the three pieces of wire at a central point above the mobile. Fix a final piece of wire at this point with which to hang the mobile. Twist this last piece of wire around a key ring or curtain ring. Make sure the mobile hangs straight.

Right: **The finished metal mobile may be hung in a tree. It creates an interesting contrast of textures against the gnarled bark.**

living ornaments

We associate ornamental features in the garden with inanimate objects. However, plants offer a whole new dimension with which to create sculptural effects, utilizing shape and form, texture and colour. Shaping plants requires an understanding of growth patterns and seasonality, and reaps long-term rewards.

Topiary is the best-known form of plant sculpting. The species most commonly used are evergreens, including box (*Buxus*), yew (*Taxus baccata*) and bay (*Laurus nobilis*),

Yew is a favourite because it is a dense evergreen that grows to a good height and responds well to hard pruning, even down to nearly ground level. The only drawback is that it grows rather slowly. However, Lawson cypress (*Chamaecyparis lawsoniana*) is quick to establish and excellent if clipped regularly to keep it within bounds. Hornbeam (*Carpinus*) is also popular. It is tall and has thick summer foliage, but its deciduous habit means that it does not have such an enclosing spacial quality as evergreens.

Above: **A cast-resin mask is brought to life with a punk hairstyle of golden sedge.**

Above centre: **Topiary is the oldest form of living sculpture.**

Above right: **A pair of blue *Cedrus atlantica* f. *glauca* are twined together to form an archway. Any growth within the arch is removed to expose the form of the trunks and to encourage bushiness on the outside.**

but many other shrubs, such as camellia, rosemary and pyracantha, can give equally interesting results.

The main role of topiary is architectural, and the art has developed to include enclosures and objects. Clipped hedges are common in formal gardens: in avenues, as screening, backdrops for statues and boundaries for parterres. Heights vary from less than 1m (3ft) to perhaps 3–4m (10–13ft), depending on the scale of the site.

Along the top of the hedge, shapes can be developed from the new season's growth. A castellated effect is possible, while figurative shapes such as birds and animals can tell a story or frame an entrance. The shape is entirely up to your imagination. Redundant hedges and overgrown bushes can be transformed into such bizarre creations as railway engines and ocean liners, rowing boats and helicopters. It is very fashionable at the moment to grow single shapes in a pot on a terrace; as topiary takes time to mature, these have the advantage that they can be taken with you if you move home.

Use hedging to develop the other forms of plant shaping, which start to become more akin to sculpture. For example, window holes cut into a hedge can open up an interesting vista beyond. A series of slots enable you to walk or look through to an adjacent area, while niches can serve to frame a sculpture or a seat.

Clipping is the way to contour dense shrubs, but other species can be trained differently. Left to their own devices, climbers tend to sprawl about quickly into a tangled mass of foliage and flower. By using a wirework frame such as a cone or a large ball, plants such as clematis, jasmine and passionflower can be formed into an elegant shape, revealing the individual blooms to perfection. Ivies can be trained in the same way to make instant evergreen obelisks planted in pots.

There are more avant-garde ways to train trees into shapes, utilizing the habit of bark to form itself over obstacles as the trunk grows in girth. Trees and shrubs can become real living sculptures. When young, all manner of trees can be twined into different shapes. You can create an archway or pergola by bending over two or more trees and tying them together where they meet. For extra panache, entwine the remaining growing points to form a ball or heart-shaped finial on top.

Architectural shapes such as obelisks, cones and spirals are useful devices for framing doorways and entrances and for use in formal parterres, where they can be used as vertical statements to emphasize the configuration of a design. In the Far East, the art of cloud topiary is popular for formal statements. This involves clipping back parts of the growth to reveal its structure while forming cloud-shaped blocks of foliage on the upper side of the bough.

Trees such as lime (*Tilia*) and hornbeam are often trained in a form known as pleaching. They are planted in line, 1–2m (3–6ft) apart, with the lower branches removed; then the upper branches are trained sideways along horizontal wires so that each tree ultimately intermingles with its neighbour. Formed into avenues, they allow a view between the clear trunks of the landscape on either side, while marking out the path with a block of foliage above.

Above left: **Conifers such as thuja and cupressus make dense, narrow forms. These two columns have been crossed over and tied together below the growing points, resulting in a strongly architectural arch.**

Above: **Individual plants, such as this *Agave americana*, make sculptural statements in their own right.**

Cloud topiary was originally created by Buddhist monks to reproduce, on a reduced scale, the asymmetrical appearance of mature, storm-ravaged pine trees. Drawing on the influences of both topiary and bonsai, cloud topiary transforms a bushy shrub into a miniature tree by using the inner framework of branches to support floating "clouds" of foliage. Cloud topiary looks striking in large decorative containers, but it is essential that you do not allow the soil to dry out.

cloud topiary

Materials and Equipment

a bushy shrub, about 60–120cm

(2–4ft) high

coloured wool (yarn) or tape

pair of secateurs (hand pruners)

Suitable Plants

Box (*Buxus sempervirens*)

Japanese holly (*Ilex crenata*)

Japanese azalea (*Rhododendron*)

Orange bark myrtle (*Myrtus

***apiculata*)**

Common myrtle (*Myrtus communis*)

Pine (*Pinus*)

Juniper (*Juniperus*)

Spruce (*Picea*)

Fir (*Abies*)

1

2

1 Choose a suitable shrub, such as box (*Buxus sempervirens*), Japanese holly (*Ilex crenata*) or other small-leaved evergreen shrubs that tolerate and respond to clipping. Large specimens from garden centres are likely to be expensive, so it is worth looking in your own garden to see if you have a suitable shrub, particularly if this is your first attempt at topiarizing. You will need to find a shrub with a good "bone" structure.

2 Open up the foliage to reveal the framework of branches. An ideal scenario is one or more main stems with strong side branches.

3 Decide which side branches to remove in order to thin out the structure. You should spend some time thinking through what you plan to do before starting to cut, and mark the ones to be retained with the coloured tape or wool (yarn). You will need to cut out approximately half the branches.

3

4

5

4 Cut out the unwanted branches, leaving behind more than you will actually need at this stage. Turn the plant around and stand back regularly to "see" the shape.

5 The individual heads of foliage can now be roughly clipped into pom-pom shapes. The clouds of foliage can eventually be developed into pom-poms or mushroom heads, although the latter is much more authentic. The individual clouds should vary in size and shape with a larger one at the top. There should also be adequate space between them.

6 Strip the leaves and smaller branches off the main branches that are to be retained.

6

7

8

7 Decide which branches or clouds are not required, but leave one or two within the framework.

8 Cut back the pom-poms quite hard to encourage dense, compact, new growth. As the piece develops, you might decide to remove individual clouds to prevent the plant from looking overcrowded. There should ideally be space between each cloud. Use wire or wooden splints to separate the branches if required.

Right: **The finished topiary clouds look absolutely spectacular against a blue, cloud-filled sky.**

Aftercare

Pruning should ideally be carried out in the spring after the threat of frosts has passed to prevent the new foliage from being burnt. Clip once or twice during the summer to maintain and improve the shape. The number of times you clip depends on the vigour of the plant. If the specimen is grown in a pot, it will need feeding as well as watering. Shrubs grown in pots are very vulnerable to drying out because they show no signs of damage until the worst has been done. Topiary is expensive and requires lots of care, so ensure that your specimen does not dry out.

There is one service that you can provide to transform your garden at a stroke, and that is to install lighting. A lit garden becomes another room, an extension of the house instead of a black hole; this is a bonus in summer but a real boon in winter, especially for gardeners far from the equator. Many garden enthusiasts have to be content with seeing the garden only at night during the working week, so the benefits stand out immediately.

lights

Right: **Candle lanterns make attractive and flexible garden lights.**

Top right: **A delicately formed, miniature, wrought-iron "candle tree" blends beautifully with the surrounding planting.**

Centre: **Low-voltage "fairy lights", wound around these metal frames, create a magical night-time effect in this vine tunnel. The addition of tiny spotlights at ground level accentuates the theme and helps to guide visitor through.**

Opposite (top): **Well-designed, stand-alone electric fittings can make a feature in their own right. This brass, mushroom-shaped downlighter marks and illuminates a flight of steps.**

Opposite (centre): **This magnificent, wrought-iron entrance gate is crowned by a splendid coach lamp in order to light the way at night.**

Light fittings are available in enormous variety and can be separated into the categories of security and display, up-lighting, flooding and highlighting. Up-lighters generally deliver the most sensitive effects, with subtlety being the key to success. Envisage the result you want, and try to achieve it with the smallest fittings available.

To guide the way along paths and to mark the edge of a pool, terrace or steps, small fixed up-lighters set into the paving blocks are subtle and attractive. They can

be used in conjunction with special effects such as glazed obelisks or wirework columns to create a formal entrance or mark a pathway. To illuminate a light-well, crushed windscreen glass spread over a broad transparent cover will hide the lamps and diffuse the light in a textural way, making it look like a pool.

Directional up-lighting works well to highlight a sculpture or to backlight a water feature; it can also make a soft

wash for the elevations of the property. Generally, trees and plants look best lit from underneath to reveal their shape and form. The appearance of a dramatically branching specimen tree illuminated at night is magnificent.

Pin-sized light beams make delightful fairy-tale effects. They can emerge in twinkling groups from hanging lanterns, be distributed like a mist through ground cover on tiny stalks, or fixed in strips to make a feature from the edges of steps.

Floodlights are easy and cheap but need to be used with care; avoid the football stadium syndrome at all costs. If you are concerned about intruders, install movement-sensitive trip switches that operate the lights only when triggered.

The perfect lighting scheme would be installed during the garden's construction, so that cabling is disguised and lamps positioned discreetly. If this is not possible, wall-mounted exterior lamps are the answer. They can be sourced in carriage-lamp style or in contemporary forms.

Ready-made sets of up-lighters that stake into the ground can be purchased from garden centres, but avoid those with lurid coloured lenses. When sited with care, the white lights are acceptable.

It must be stressed that electricity needs to be firmly and securely separated from water, wet soil and garden users. A qualified expert must make electricity connections to the main house, and any large installation is a job for professionals.

Candlelight is the gentlest and perhaps the best way to create ambience. Tea lights are cheap; set them in jam jars or hanging tin lanterns, line them up steps and along walls. Regular candles are best used in glass hurricane lamps to keep them from breezes. The nicest ones are hand blown, tall and set on high necks. However, all kinds of candelabra look romantic in the garden, and the running wax just adds to the baroque effect. Special garden candles have thick wicks that stay alight even in a storm; these create smoke and should never be used indoors. Candle or oil-burning torches to push into the ground are great for parties and big entrances.

Water is a fundamental element of life. Our bodies are almost completely composed of it, and all living things rely totally on water to exist. So, it should be no surprise that water has such a sublime effect on our spirits. When trickling or bubbling, water is soothing, while the energy and noise of a crashing cascade can be stimulating. This is an important quality to consider, as there is a world of difference between the relaxing effect of slow-moving water and the insistent noise of a dynamic installation.

water features

Right: **Light-filled droplets are one of the loveliest features of moving water. Rather oversized for bathing, a peacock looks on with disdain.**

architectural features, there can be so many distractions that the main point of focus is lost. Water, with its inherent vibrancy, creates a cool, visual gap with qualities very different from those of inert paving. In a controlled design, a rectangular pool could substitute for a gravel parterre, whereas in less formal surroundings, a simple pond would be appropriate. The physical and sensual qualities of water are the same, whether it is formally controlled in a restricted space or allowed to range freely over a large area. However, the resulting impression will be very different in these diverse situations.

The spatial qualities of water in garden design are often overlooked at the planning stage. Water surfaces reflect light, introducing a unique creative dimension. A still pool mirrors trees and shadows, while even the slightest breeze brings flickering images and fragments of brightness. These are useful devices to enliven a shady area.

In areas of dense or busy planting, there is a danger of a kind of visual indigestion. Where there are a lot of competing

Top: **This is a simple idea and looks so stunning. Thin copper pipes emerge, reed-like, from the pond to release fine jets of water through the dappled sunlight.**

Left: **This is a simple and effective idea that can easily be adapted to suit a wide variety of styles by changing the base receptacle and the style of the spout.**

It is probable that the majority of us have to be content with a small water feature in our garden, and consequently it is likely to be of a more formal nature. It is possible to buy ready-made pieces, but they have limited scope with results tending towards the banal. Small, self-contained units often look like superfluous bits of decoration. The reason is simply that, if water is to be successful, it needs to be treated as part of the landscaping design, built into the construction, not placed on the surface.

Left: **This cascade over a wall is designed to look as though it falls from a stream on a higher level. It has, in fact, been created with the help of a pump that recirculates the water from the reservoir below.**

Below left: **A small, carved gargoyle, set in a niche, releases a steady flow of water into a shallow stone stoup.**

Once you start to play with the idea of moving water, you begin to see more and more possibilities. One thing to remember is that, whatever the scale of the water project, the principle of the system remains the same. A holding situation at the lowest level is filled with water where the pump is situated; the pump circulates the water by pushing it up to the highest point, from where it will descend to the bottom again. An electricity supply, which should be installed professionally to meet exterior standards, is required, and thought should be given to hiding the pump and the cable.

Results are invariably more interesting if a special design is created using attractive elements. Even in its simplest incarnation, a hand-carved bowl will make a birdbath or an elegant dish in which to float flowers.

Architectural salvage yards are great sources for water troughs, carved bowls, pool edging, masks and fountain statuary. Landscape suppliers can provide rocks and stones, while specialist garden stores offer lead, terracotta and stone containers.

Above: **Wall fountains can be created in many different styles. This has been built to match the wall, using local flints, and, being in an area where there are a number of ecclesiastical buildings, it includes a relic from a derelict church.**

Left: **Water channels can be adapted to both classical and contemporary designs. This is part of a large system that was created by William Kent in the 18th century.**

Wall fountains are a good choice where space is limited, and this is an area where a self-contained design can be employed. However, you can have fun designing your own. A mask provides the opportunity for a spout to emerge from its mouth. Water collects in bowl below for circulation. It need not be figurative at all, the emphasis being placed entirely on the container. An oversized stone or lead cistern could stand alone with just a bold spout to release the water. The scale can vary from tiny to immense, and the force of water adapted to suit the design.

For a bigger splash, create a cascade. Instead of a spout in the wall, create a horizontal slot, 1–2m (3–6ft) wide, from which water can crash in one continuous surge. This obviously needs professional installation and a special site, preferably one with plenty of space in an area with changing levels. It would be perfect beside a swimming pool, where it could gush out from an adjacent retaining wall.

Even without the need for complicated plumbing, you can easily create a stylish display yourself. Choose an attractive watertight container, deep enough to

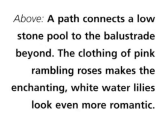

Above: **A path connects a low stone pool to the balustrade beyond. The clothing of pink rambling roses makes the enchanting, white water lilies look even more romantic.**

Top centre: **A grand tier of waterfalls completes this neo-classical design. The construction of riven stone and slates gives it a sense of drama and power to complement the villa and gateway.**

contain the pump. If the container is tall, the pump can be supported on bricks to bring it close to the surface, or in the case of a shallow form, it can be hidden by stones to become part of the finished design. In a small feature like this, a low-powered pump is adequate to allow the water to bubble gently up to the surface.

Many more designs can be developed from this idea. For example, the Ali Baba garden urn makes a shapely form out of

which water can flow. You will need to excavate a level-based pit about 10cm (4in) deep. In the centre, dig a deep hole to contain a reservoir in which to put the pump. Seal the whole area with heavy-duty plastic or obtain a suitably shaped plastic liner. Place the urn over the reservoir, supported securely on horizontal struts, and cover the ground surface with pebbles. The pump will push the water from the reservoir up a pipe taken through the drainage hole in the pot, forcing it to cascade over the rim and on to the pebbles.

simplest, naturalistic effects to achieve, suiting itself to both formal and rustic situations. However, as water pumps increase in sophistication, you can have several outlets controlled to "jump" up and down at different heights.

Sprinkling fountain-style jets are regarded as the garden classic, but these need a decent amount of space in a formal setting to avoid looking kitsch. It is possible to make a smaller-scale version; you can use jets that force water droplets up and round from a central point to create a low, recurved dome.

Water can be pushed up to emerge in three distinct ways. It can come up in a vertical jet resulting in a single dynamic geyser, but this is really only effective on an enormous scale in a lake. Better to create a broader, vertical bubbling effect, varying in height from a few inches to perhaps 1m (3ft). This is the most versatile, because pumps allow you to alter the velocity to control the effect you require. Low surface movement over rocks is one of the

Above: **A low-powered jet disturbs the surface of a rectangular pool bordered by flat stone slabs. The bronze cats sits wistfully, hoping for an imaginary goldfish.**

Centre bottom: **The boundary of standard-trained trees, which appear to have to cope with a permanently prevailing wind, give a sense of containment and shelter to this stone-walled pool.**

Left: **It is always refreshing to see humorous touches in the garden; these welded steel crows disgorge water from their huge bills.**

Below left: **Mythological gods are perennial favourites for water gardens.**

Below centre: **The transparent and light-reflecting qualities of glass work well with water.**

Below right: **Carved granite balls combine excellently with the gentle trickle of water falling over them. These would work well in either a contemporary or Japanese design.**

Capitalize on water's gravitational urge to run down from a high level to a succession of collecting points below. Steps are an obvious example, and lend themselves to a contemporary garden, where water running down slabs of white limestone set off by borders of black slate could make a transition from a terrace to a pool below.

It is possible to adapt designs to suit any style simply by changing the components. For a woodland effect on a slope, "steps" can be composed of large rocks over which water can either crash dramatically or trickle gently. Instead of falling water, it can be induced into a shallow stream bedded with gleaming river pebbles or black slate

fragments. Slate is a lovely stone to use with water because its green, grey and black tones complement water perfectly; it can even be used without water to present the image of a running stream.

The linear progression of a stream can be utilized to divide a garden into areas or to differentiate between levels. This idea

Right: **A small battalion of indignant carp defend their side of the stream from intruders.**

Below left: **This trio of columns of slate discs makes an effective visual statement, highlighted in the sunshine by water spilling down the sides.**

Below centre: **In this engaging sculpture, a tousle-haired water carrier deftly supports a shallow bowl above a leaden tank.**

Below right: **Brilliant blue and turquoise tiles give a Mediterranean feel to this tiny pool in a terracotta courtyard.**

works excellently in a formal situation when water fills narrow channels bordered by paving slabs to bring visual relief. If on a single level, it may be static but shallow level changes can be accommodated too. Bear in mind, though, that the resulting mini waterfalls would need to be controlled by a pump.

If you hanker for living art, give your creative energies full reign and make a dashing water sculpture. This could involve a series of vessels with water cascading from one vessel to the next. A central, free-standing, hollow steel tube could allow the water to pass upwards, releasing it from the top into collecting

cups arranged down its length. If this type of water feature appeals to you, it is important to consider that some technical skill will be required to create it. Our project for a steel water feature on pages 152–153 will provide inspiration for a similar design and is a simple idea that can be adapted to your own garden.

steel water feature

This stylish, contemporary water feature is made from three stainless steel tubes. The water tumbles from slits in the tubes as well as over the top and down the sides of each one. Other materials, such as terracotta, plastic and copper, could also be used. The splashing sound can be "tuned" by adjusting the water pressure.

Materials and Equipment

plastic reservoir tank, about 600mm
(24in) wide and 600mm (24in) deep

sand/geotextile fleece

polythene (plastic) pond liner

submersible water pump (maximum
flow 3720 litres/819 gallons per hour)

25mm (1in) galvanized metal grille

fine plastic shade netting

plastic water pipe, 25mm (1in)
in diameter

plastic water pipe, 13mm (½in)
in diameter

3 x 13mm (½in) flow taps

5 x 25mm (1in) clips

three-way T-piece

3 x 100sq mm (1.5sq in) stainless steel
tubes, 800mm (31in), 1000mm
(39in) and 1200mm (48in) high

25mm (1in) to 13mm (½in)

shovel

hacksaw

screwdriver

wire cutters

1

2

Preparation

A steel fabricator should be able to supply you with some stainless steel tube. The cheapest option is to use standard-size pipes. Here, we used 100sq mm (1.5sq in) pipes in three cut lengths of 800mm (31in), 1000mm (39in) and 1200mm (48in), with a base plate and 13mm (½in) inlet pipe welded to each pipe. The pipes were bead-blasted to give a matt finish. To cut the slots into the pipes you can use a quality hacksaw. The ideal height for the slots is 50–100mm (2–4in) from the top of the pipes – any further from the top and the water will flow out too far.

1 Clear and level an area approximately 1800sq m (72sq in) to a depth of about 50mm (2in) with sloping sides. Within the cleared area, dig a hole approximately 600mm (24in) by 600mm (24in), or large enough to suit the size of reservoir. Ask a qualified electrician to dig a trench for the power supply, for which you will need an outdoor socket or waterproof junction box. Insert the container in the hole, making sure it is level and flush with the cleared area. Backfill with soil or sand if necessary.

2 Once the reservoir is level, line the cleared area and reservoir with geotextile fleece or sand. Using a sharp knife, cut a hole in the fleece above the reservoir.

3 Lay the pond liner over the fleece and the reservoir. Gradually add the water to the reservoir in order to pull the liner into place, remembering to fold the liner flat over the cleared area. Stand the stainless steel pipes on top of the liner next to the reservoir, in the desired configuration, making sure the pipes are vertical.

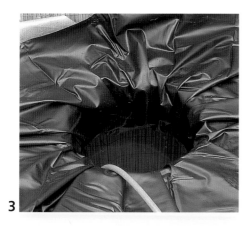

3

4

5

6

4 Place the pump in the reservoir and cover with the galvanized metal grille. Cut out a hole for the pipe to pass through.

5 To keep back finer particles, cover the metal grille with fine plastic shade netting.
6 Connect up the 25mm (1in) hose to the pump secured by a clip and connect the other end to the 25mm (1in) to 13mm (½in) three-way T-piece. Connect each of the outlet pipes to the 13mm (½in) hose and flow taps, which are then connected and secured with clips to the inlet pipes on each of the steel tubes. Cover over with cobbles, rocks and gravel. Turn on the power and adjust the flow of water as required.

Care and Maintenance

Evaporation will reduce the water supply, but the reservoir can be easily topped up by pouring water through the cobbles. There are a number of chemical products available for recirculating water features which keeps them free from algal growth.

Warning

Ask a qualified electrician to install all the outdoor sockets, switches and circuit breakers that are required for this feature.

Templates

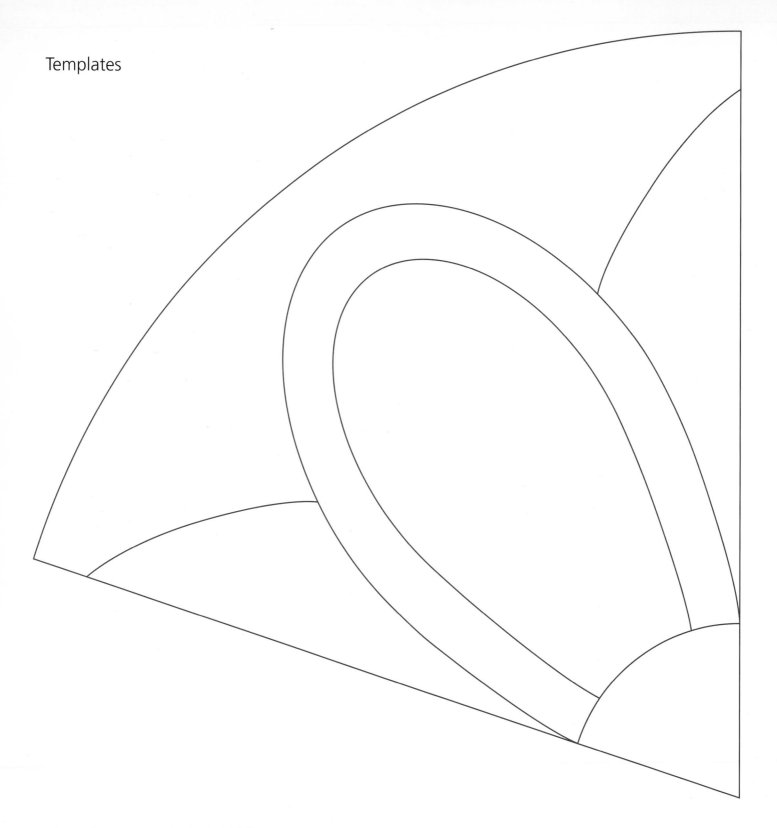

To make the Mosaic Table featured on pages 108–111, you will need to enlarge the template above by 146% on a photocopier. This template represents a one-fifth segment of the whole mosaic design, so you will need to enlarge five templates and tape them together.

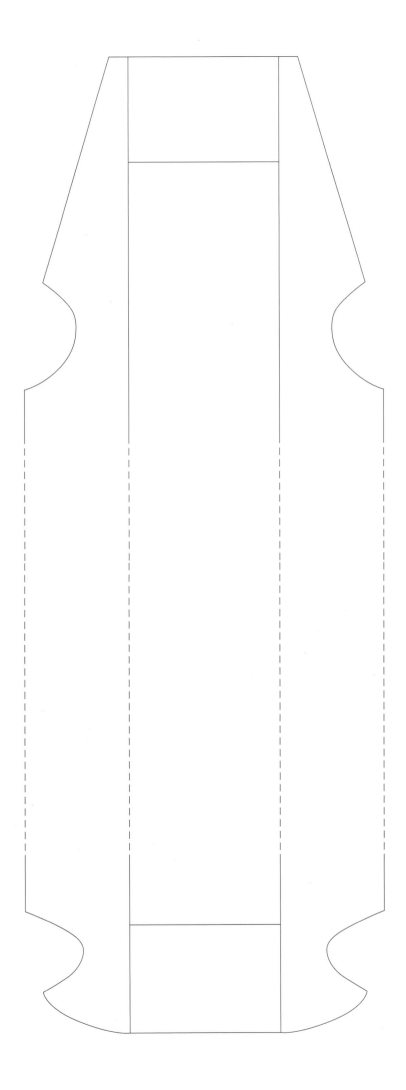

To make the Willow and Hazel Pig featured on pages 126–129, you will need to enlarge the template above by 250% on a photocopier. It is recommended that you use the template for the head and rear of the pig only. The dotted lines serve to represent the actual length of the pig measured from the front to the back legs. This measurement should be 45cm (18in). The distance between the two pieces of wood should be 10cm (4in).

Suppliers

UNITED KINGDOM

Avant Garden

London W4 2RH

Tel: 0208 747 1794

Fax: 0208 994 0793

sales@avantgarden.co.uk

www.avantgarden.co.uk

Architectural ornament,

planters, topiary frames.

By appointment and

mail order.

Contact Joan Clifton.

(The items that are featured

on page 3/top and 158–159

are all available from

Avant Garden.)

Brampton Willows

Upper Farm

Brampton

Beccles

Suffolk NR34 8EH

Tel: 01502 575891

Fax: 01502 575489

Willow structures .

Gaze Burvill

Newtonwood Workshop

Newton Valence

Alton

Hampshire

GU34 3EW

Tel: 01420 587467

FaxL 01420 587354

gazeburvil@aol.com

Oak furniture.

Civil Engineering

Developments

728 London Road

West Thurrock

Grays, Essex RM20 3LU

Tel: 01708 867237

Pebbles, gravel and boulders.

Local depots and mail order.

Tom Clark

18 Church Street

Martock

Somerset TA12 6JL

Tel: 01935 822111

Fax: 01935 825809

Stone carving and sculpture.

Joan Clifton

Horticouture

London W4 2RH

Tel: 0208 747 1794

Fax: 0208 994 0793

www.horticouture.com

By appointment.

Design consultancy.

Crowther of Syon Lodge

Busch Corner

London Road

Isleworth TW7 5BH

Tel: 020 8560 7978

Fax: 0208 568 7572

crowther.syon-

lodge@virgin.net

www.crowther-syon-

lodge.co.uk

Antique garden ornament.

Fantails

Dorset

Tel: 01929 427676

Fax: 01929 421509

fantails@freenetname.co.uk

www.fantails.co.uk

Mail order.

Contact Des Bennett.

Adirondack furniture.

Fire and Iron Gallery

Rowhurst Forge

Oxshott Road

Leatherhead

Surrey KT22 0EN

Tel and Fax: 01372 386453

www.fireandiron.co.uk

Contact Lucy Quinnell.

Ironwork and sculpture.

Forsham Cottage Arks

Goreside Farm

Great Chart

Ashford

Kent TN26 1JU

Tel: 01233 820229

Fax: 01233 820157

S & B Evans & Sons

7a Ezra Street

London E2 7RH

Tel: 0207 729 6635

Fax: 0207 613 3558

By appointment. Terracotta.

Dennis Fairweather

Fairweather Sculpture

Norfolk

fairweather.sculpture@tinyon-

line.co.uk

By appointment.

David Harber Sundials

The Sundial Workshop

Valley Farm

Bix, Henley-on-Thames

Oxfordshire RG9 6BW

Tel: 01491 576956

Fax: 01491 413524

sales@davidharbersundials.co.uk

LASSCO

Saint Michaels

Mark Street

London EC2A 4ER

Tel: 020 77390448

Fax: 020 7729 6853

lassco@zetnet.co.uk

www.lassco.co.uk

Architectural reclamation.

Lister Lutyens
Company Limited
Hammonds Drive
Eastbourne
East Sussex BN23 6PW
Tel: 01323 431177
Fax: 01323 639314
SALES@lister-lutyens.demon.co.uk

Lizzard
Manor House
Saxby, Melton Mowbray
Leicestershire LE14 2RR
Tel: 01572 787 503
Fax: 01572 787 688
Bronze fountains & sculpture.

Christopher Marvell
The Old Rising Sun
Apthorpe Street
Fulbourn, Cambridge
Cambridgeshire CB1 5EY
chris@marvell.abelgratis.net
Sculpture.

Read's Nurseries
Hales Hall
Lodden
Norwich NR14 6QW
Tel: 01508 548395
Catalogue and mail order.

Redwood Stone
The Stoneworks
West Horrington
Wells BA5 3EH
Somerset
Tel: 01749 677777
Fax: 01749 671177

sales@redwoodstone.co.uk
Stone ornament.

The Romantic Garden Nursery
Swannington
Norwich
Norfolk YO18 7HG
Tel: 01603 261488
Fax: 01603 864231
enquires@romantic-garden.demon.co.uk
Topiary.

Helen Sinclair
Sculpture Culture
Rhossili Farmhouse
Rhossili
Swansea SA3 1PL
Tel and Fax: 01792 390798

UNITED STATES

Gardener's Supply Company
128 Intervale Road
Burlington, VT 05401
Tel: (800) 863-1700
www.gardeners.com

Garden Oaks Specialties
1921 Route 22 West
Bound Brook, NJ08805
Tel: (732) 356-7333
Fax: (732) 356-7202
www.gardenoaks.com

Bear Creek Lumber
P.O. Box 669
Winthrop, WA 98862
Tel: (800) 597-7191
Fax: (509) 997-2040
www.bearcreeklumber.com

High Plains Stone
P.O. Box 100
Castle Rock, CO 80104
Tel: (303) 791-1862
www.highplainsstone.com

The Home Depot
www.HomeDepot.com

Lowe's Home Improvement
Warehouse
www.lowes.com

Plant Delights Nursery, Inc.
9241 Sauls Road
Raleigh, NC 27603
Tel: (919) 772-4794
Fax: (919) 662-0370
www.plantdel.com

AUSTRALIA

Jardinique
Shop 6
Reginald Street
CREMORNE NSW 2090
Tel: (02) 9908 7000

The Parterre Garden
33 Ocean Street
WOOLLAHRA NSW 2025
Tel: (02) 9363 5874
Fax (02) 9327 8466
527 Military Road
MOSMAN NSW 2088
Tel: (02) 9960 5900
Fax: (02) 9960 5700

Cotswold Garden Furniture
42 Hotham Parade
Artarmon NSW 2064
Tel: (02) 9906 5417
Fax: (02) 9906 5417

Porter's Original Paints
Distributed in all states
895 Bourke Street
WATERLOO NSW 2017
Tel: 02 9698 5322

Whitehouse Gardens
388 Springvale Road
FOREST HILL VIC 3131
Tel and Fax: (03) 9877 1430

Index

Page numbers in *italics* refer to illustrations.

ACKNOWLEDGEMENTS

Publisher's Acknowledgements

The publishers would like to thank the following garden owners, designers and institutions for allowing their gardens to be photographed for this book. All photographs were taken by Jo Whitworth, unless stated otherwise.

t = top   b = bottom   c = centre
l = left   r = right

Amberley Japanese Garden, nr. Beaworthy, Devon 62r; 63r

Baggy House (architects: Hudson Featherstone, London) 76t; 104bl; 105bl

Brook Hall (designers: Prof. Keith Hopkins and Dr. Jennifer Hopkins) 42r; 21bl; 23cr; 47tr; 87br; 95cl

Chelsea Flower Show, 1999 16 ('The Sensory Garden'/designer: Claire Whitehouse); 21tl ('Horti-Couture'/ designer: James Alexander-Sinclair); 22 and 23cl (bottom) ('Help the Aged World Life Garden/designer: Naila Green); 23tr; 28r; 34 l and c ('Sculpture in the Garden'/designer: George Carter); 42l 'My Retreat'/designer: Andrew Bond); 61tc (photographer: Jonathan Buckley); 70 ('A Floating Garden'/designer: Paul Cooper); 73tr ('The Daily Telegraph Reflective Garden'/ designer: Michael Baston); 76b (photographer: Jonathan Buckley); 79b (Courtyard Garden, Pembrokeshire Horticultural Society); 79b (Courtyard Garden, Pembrokeshire Horticultural Society); 85t ('Help the Aged World Life Garden'/designer: Naila Green); 104tl ('Mr. McGregor's Garden'/designer: Jacquie Gordon); 104br ('21st Century Street'/ designer: Carol Klein); 105tr (Selsdon & District Horticultural Society); 105br 'My Retreat'/ designer: Andrew Bond); 112br (photographer: Jonathan Buckley); 113b (photographer: Jonathan Buckley); 114 ('The Chef's Roof Garden/designer: Terence Conran); 122t (photographer: Jonathan Buckley); 124tl (photographer: Jonathan Buckley); 125tr (photographer: Jonathan Buckley); 138l (photographer: Jonathan Buckley); 139r; 147t (photographer: Jonathan Buckley); 149r ('Mr McGregor's Garden'/designer: Jacquie Gordon); 150bl (Redwood Stone, Wells, Somerset); 151br (photographer: Jonathan Buckley)

The Coppice, Reigate, Surrey 95cr (photographer: Jonathan Buckley)

East Ruston Old Vicarage, Norwich 37b; 38l; 39bl; 78bl; 83t; 86tc; 89c; 104tr; 145r

Forge Cottage, Jaspers Green (designer: Carolynn Blythe) 20; 21bc; 23bl; 29tl; 46tl; 66tl; 79tr; 82tr

Fairweather Sculpture, Hillside House, Startston, Norfolk (garden designer and sculptor: Dennis Fairweather) 124tr; 125tl and tc; 138l; 151blc

Fovant Hut, Wiltshire (designer: Christina Oates) 3bl; 46br; 69tr; 83cl; 84t; 89r

The Garden in Mind, Hampshire (designer: Ivan Hicks) 3br; 5b; 9l; 9c; 61tl; 130b; 131t; 138r; 139c

Will Giles, Oak Tree House, Norwich 103b; 147cr

Hampton Court Flower Show, 1999 13l, 21tc and 23cl (top) ('Anglo Aquarium Plant Garden', designer: Jane Sweetser); 23tl; 25c ('Feng Shui Garden'/sculptor: Janis Ridley); 43 ('Feng Shui Garden'/designer: Pamela Woods); 62t (sculptor: Dennis Fairweather); 94t ('A Safe Haven Garden'/designer: Ruth Chivers); 113cr ('A Safe Haven Garden'/ designer: Ruth Chivers); 115c (Beachcomber Trading Ltd. Herts.); 150t ('Merlin's Water Garden'/designer: Graham Robb); 150c ('A Safe Haven Garden'/ designer: Ruth Chivers); 151t ('Merlin's Water Garden'/designer: Graham Robb); 151bl; 156 ('Anglo Aquarium Plant Garden'/designer: Jane Sweetser)

The Hannah Peschar Sculpture Garden, Black and White Cottage, Ockley, Surrey (designed by Anthony Paul, Landscape Designer) 11cl (bottom) and 14t ('Winged Arch' by Stephanie Burn); 13bc (wood-carving in oak by Walter Bailey); 24 ('Amongst Words and Phrases' by Mark Clayne Frith); 25l; 60t ('Sit' by Hannah Peschar); 60b (bridge designed by Anthony Paul); 78br and 133l ('Vein II' by Lucien Simon); 88l (reclaimed steps by Anthony Paul); 102cr (deck designed by Antony Paul/stoneware by Jennifer Jones); 105tl; 112br; 130t ('Pictish Spiral Bench' by Nigel Ross); 131b ('Trunks' by Giles Kent); 132c ('Organic Form' by Peter Clarke); 132r ('King and Queen' by Helen Sinclair); 133c and 133r ('Euridice' by Helen Sinclair); 146t ('Swaylines' by Andrew Ewing)

Heale House Garden, Middle Woodford, nr. Salisbury SP4 6NT, tel: 91722 782504 (open to the public) 23tc; 29tc; 61tr; 61cl; 86br; 115r; 87tr; 112bl; 148l

Hillbarn House, Great Bedwyn, Wiltshire 47tl; 89b

Iford Manor, Bradford-on-Avon, Wiltshire 3tl; 15br; 23br; 28c; 32; 33; 39r; 58b; 78t; 86bl; 122c; 122b; 123cr; 124tc; 146b; 147cl

Le Manoir aux Quat' Saisons, Oxon 47br; 59b; 124b; 94c; 146c

Little Cottage, Lymington 79tc; 150bl

The New Art Centre Sculpture Park & Gallery, Roche Court, nr. Salisbury, Wiltshire 92t ('Moonstone III' by Meical Watts); 92b ('Inceptis Gravibus' by Brenda Berman and Annet Stirling); 93tl ('Initial Posts' by Martin Jennings); 93tr ('Found Letter's by Alex Peever); 93bl ('Hermetic Numerals' by John Das Gupta); 93br ('WB Yeats Table' by James Salisbury); 132l ('Butterfly Gate' by Victoria Rance)

Osler Road, Oxford (designers: Mr. and Mrs. N. Coote) 90l and r; 40; 91tl and bl; 112t

Painswick Rococco Garden, Painswick, Glos 36t

RHS Gardens, Wisley 28t

Starston Hall, Norfolk (designer: Christina Baxter) 11br; 21br; 82bl

St. Regis Close, London N10 (designers: S. Bennett and E. Hyde/garden is open under National Gardens Scheme) 102b

Tatton Park, RHS Flower Show, 1999 ('Oasis in the Urban Jungle'/designer: Jan Williams) 77r

Julia van den Bosch's garden, Ham, London 17l; 27t; 102t; 157

West Green House Garden, near Hartney Wintney, Hampshire 5t; 7b; 11lb; 18r; 95b; 97b; 115l; 144t (garden owner and designer: Marylynn Abbott).

Gay Wilson (garden designer) 33 Balmuir Gardens, Putney, London 18bl; 82c; 102cl; 103t

Diana Yakeley (garden designer), 13 College Cross, Islington, London 9r; 11tr; 30c; 35r; 79tl; 103cr; 113t

The publishers would also like to thank the following picture agencies and photographers for allowing their images to be reproduced for this book:

EWA = Elizabeth Whiting Associates
GPL = The Garden Picture Library

1 Jonathan Buckley (designer: Susan Sharkey, Brentford, England/Sculptor: Dennis Fairweather); 2 Jonathan Buckley (Dolwen, Llanrhaeadr, Wales); 3tc GPL (Mark Bolton); 3tr EWA (Beckley Park, Oxon); 3bc EWA (The Water Gardens, Kingston Hill); 6 EWA; 7t Houses & Interiors (Steve Sparrow); 7c GPL (Steven Wooster); 8 EWA; 10t EWA; 10b GTRE/ John Glover (Tresco Abbey Gardens, Isles of Scilly); 11tl EWA; 11lc (top) EWA (Beckley Park, Oxon); 12 EWA; 13r GPL (Christopher Gallagher); 14b Bruce Coleman Collection/ Derek Croucher (Chateau Chenonceau, France); 15t Wildlife Matters (The Blue Steps, Naumkeag, Massachusetts, USA/ designer: Fletcher Steele); 15bl GPL (Ron Evans); 15bc Houses & Interiors (Mark Bolton); 17c Chelsea Flower Show, 1997 (Yves St Laurent Garden/designer: Madison Cox); 17r GPL (JS Sira); 18tl Jonathan Buckley (designer: Anthony Noel); 19 GPL (Michael Paul); 25r Bruce Coleman Collection (Kim Taylor); 26t Jonathan Buckley (Pashley Manor, Sussex); 26b GPL (Steven Wooster); 27bA-Z Botanical Collection Ltd. (Darryl Sweetland); 28bl Jonathan Buckley (Church Lane, London/ designer: PaulKelly); 29tr Sutton Place, Guildford, Surrey; 29b A-Z Botanical Collection Ltd. (Derrick Ditchburn); 30t Wildlife Matters (S. California, USA/ designer: Isabelle Green); 30b GDJ/John Glover (Derek Jarman's garden, Kent); 31 EWA (La Mortella, Italy); 36b GPL/JS Sira (Ham House, Surrey); 36c GPL (Henk Dijkman); 37t GPL (Ron Sutherland); 38t GPL (Howard Rice); 40 EWA; 41 GPL (Clay Perry); 42c EWA; 44 GPL/Brigitte Thomas (Villandry, France); 45t GPL/John Glover (Hadspen House, Somerset); 45c GPL/John Glover (Preen Manor, Shropshire); 45 Houses & Interiors (Mark Bolton); 46bl GPL (Claire Davies);48 EWA; 49 EWA; 50t EWA; 50c GPL (Roger Hyam); 50b EWA; 51t GPL (Roger Hyam); 51c EWA; 51b EWA; 52tl EWA; 52bl Houses & Interiors (Steve Sparrow); 52r EWA; 53t EWA; 53b EWA; 54t EWA; 54b EWA; 55 EWA; 56 EWA; 57 GPL (John Glover); 58t Houses & Interiors (Sandra Ireland); 59t EWA; 61c EWA; 61bc EWA (The Water Gardens, Kingston Hill); 65 EWA; 66tc Garden & Wildlife Matters (Derek Jarman's garden, Kent); 66b GDS/ John Glover (Derek Jarman's garden, Kent); 67tr Garden Exposures Picture Library (Andrea Jones); 67b GDS/John Glover (Derek Jarman's garden, Kent); 68tl Simon Kenny/ Belle/Arcaid (Rottnest Island, Australia/ designer: Larry Eastwood); 68r GPL (Jerry Pavia); 69br Simon Kenny/Belle/Arcaid (Rottnest Island, Australia/designer: Larry Eastwood); 64 and 68bl (Spike Powell, © copyright Anness Publishing Ltd.); 71 Jonathan Buckley; 72tl 68tl Simon Kenny/ Belle/Arcaid (designer: Garth Barnett); 72bl GPL (Gil Hanly); 72c GPL/Steven Wooster (Chelsea Flower Show, 1999); 73br GPL (Ron Sutherland); 74tl EWA; 74cl Garden & Wildlife Matters ('Cognoscenti Garden', Hampton Court Flower Show, 1996/ designed by Duncan Heather); 74bl Geoff Lung/Arcaid (Sydney, Australia/architect: Luigi Rosselli); 74r Nicholas Kane/Arcaid (designers: Robert Sakula and Cany Ash); 75 GPL/Steven Wooster (designer: Michelle Osborne); 80bl GPL/Ron Sutherland (designer: Anthony Paul); 80c S & O Mathews (Conholt Park); 81tr EWA; 82br GPL (Lamontagne); 83cr GPL (Eric Crichton); 83b EWA; 84b GPL (Howard Rice); 85b Houses & Interiors (Sarah Ireland); 88r EWA; 89t EWA; 91tr and 91bc Jonathan Buckley (Lyndhurst Square, London/designer: Josephine Pickett-Baker); 91br Jonathan Buckley (16 Prospect Road, Warwickshire); 94b S & O Mathews; 96 S &O Mathews (Old Place Farm); 103cl Garden & Wildlife Matters (bench designer: Gaze Burvill); 112br Jonathan Buckley; 123t GPL (Juliette Wade); 138l see trannie 5; 144l GPL (Michael Howes); 144b EWA; 145t GPL (John Glover); 148tr GPL (Ron Sutherland); 148br EWA

PROJECT CONTRIBUTORS

Rosie Brister, Speckled Hen Cottage, 27 Chapel Street, Stoke-by-Clare, Tel: 01787 278932
Willow and Hazel Pig (pp.126–129) and Hazel Obelisk (pp.98–101)

George Carter, Silverstone Farm, North Elmham, Norfolk NR20 5EX, Tel: 01362 668130
Metal-Trimmed Planter (pp.118–121)

Ivan Hicks, Garden House, Stanstead Park Rowland's Castle, Hampshire PO9 6DX Tel: 01705 413149
Cloud Topiary (pp. 140–143)

John Libert, End Cottage, 66 Old Road Wateringbury, Tel: 01622 820595
Metal Mobile (pp. 134-137)

Ben Pike, Round Trees, Smallway Congresbury, North Somerset BS49 6AA Tel: 01934 876355
Steel Water Feature (pp. 152–153)

Mary Rawlinson, 1 Bower Gardens Salisbury, Wiltshire SP1 2RL Tel: 01722 321745 *Tree Seat (pp. 106–107)*

Tabby Riley, 15 Dumont Road, London N16 ONR, Tel: 0171 241 6629
Painted Pots (pp.116–117) and Mosaic Table (pp.108–111)